MUY BUENO

THREE GENERATIONS OF AUTHENTIC MEXICAN FLAVOR

· ·

RECIPES · STORIES

To our family and friends
who cheered us on!
Buen provecho!

~Vangie, Veronica
& Yvette

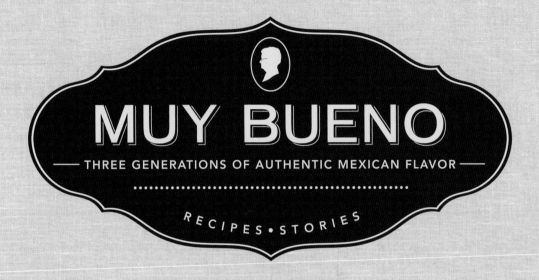

MUY BUENO

THREE GENERATIONS OF AUTHENTIC MEXICAN FLAVOR

RECIPES • STORIES

Yvette Marquez-Sharpnack :: Veronica Gonzalez-Smith :: Evangelina Soza

Photography by Jeanine Thurston

Hippocrene Books
New York

Second printing, 2013.

Copyright © 2012 Yvette Marquez-Sharpnack, Veronica Gonzalez-Smith, and Evangelina Soza.

For more information, address:
HIPPOCRENE BOOKS, INC.
171 Madison Avenue
New York, NY 10016
www.hippocrenebooks.com

Color photographs by **Jeanine Thurston**
Book and jacket design by **Yvette Marquez-Sharpnack**

Library of Congress Cataloging-in-Publication Data

Marquez-Sharpnack, Yvette.
  Muy Bueno: Three Generations of Authentic Mexican Flavor / Yvette Marquez-Sharpnack,
Veronica Gonzalez-Smith, Evangelina Soza; photography by Jeanine Thurston.
  p. cm.
  Includes index.
  ISBN 978-0-7818-1304-4 (pbk.)
  ISBN 0-7818-1304-2 (pbk.)
1. Cooking, Mexican. I. Gonzalez-Smith, Veronica. II. Soza, Evangelina.
III. Title.
  TX716.M4M374 2012
  641.5972--dc23
                        2012024173

Printed in the United States of America.

contents

three generations
of authentic mexican flavor

old-world northern mexican cuisine
1st generation ~ Jesusita

south of the border home-style dishes
2nd generation ~ Vangie

latin fusion
3rd generation ~ Veronica & Yvette

The silhouettes on each page denote whom the story or memory is from.

Chile glossary on page 17

introduction

muy bueno

When people ask us why we named our blog and cookbook *Muy Bueno*, our response is that our mother/grandmother (Grandma Jesusita) would always invite family and friends to her table with the same words: *"Siéntate a comer, esta muy bueno"* (Sit down and eat, it's very good). And she lingered on the *"muuuuy bueno"* with a smile, raised eyebrows, and a twinkle in her eyes as if to let her guests know they were in for a treat. Those two words—and the memory of Grandma and her legendary meals—never fail to bring smiles to our faces too.

Grandma was a fixture in the kitchen, preparing a delicious meal to feed whoever walked through her door. From the first bite, the lucky recipients of her efforts tasted not only the food, but Grandma's very heart and soul in everything she prepared. Not a day went by that she didn't make *frijoles de la olla*, homemade tortillas, and fresh salsa. There was always a meal on the stove, in the slow cooker, or in the oven. She would feed everyone who visited and somehow the food never ran out. Like the miracle of the five loaves and two fishes, how she fed so many visitors still remains a mystery. Her warm, inviting home with friends and relatives in place at her kitchen table is a vision that lives fondly in our memories.

Muy Bueno began between the three of us as a way to preserve favorite family recipes and stories about our childhoods and how we celebrated the more traditional holidays. However, as we began to dig deeper into our ancestral roots, we were reawakened to a rich heritage of traditional Mexican holidays and customs. In an effort to reclaim and preserve lost holiday traditions and educate our own children, we have included our most treasured pictures, recipes, and stories in this cookbook.

After our Grandma passed away, we asked Mom if we could each have one of Grandma's rolling pins. Grandma made everything from tortillas to *empanadas* with her little wooden rolling pins, and having one made us feel like she was still nearby. I can only imagine how many hours she must have spent using each of them, and I know if the rolling pins could talk, they'd have some good stories to tell! We hope to log more hours on each, making all our favorite family recipes with our own kids. One day our children will inherit the rolling pins and they too will have their own sweet memories to carry with them.

We are not professionally trained cooks nor do we claim to have the best Mexican recipes. These recipes are simply our family's recipes. Along this journey, we've learned a thing or two about cooking, and every once in a while we get an idea for a new recipe. Thanks to Grandma Jesusita, who we know is watching over us, we feel that maybe, just maybe, she whispers a few words of encouragement into our ears to help us find our way around the kitchen and turn out a recipe worthy of her praise.

Some memories, like watching Grandma rolling her delicious tortillas and making her famous salsas and enchiladas, are still so vivid. And some, like the times we spent with all our cousins on Christmas Eve and large family barbecues, are the most difficult to convey to our children since nowadays our family is scattered around the globe. We wanted to capture the spirit, warmth, love, and flavor of our beautiful Mexican-American family in this cookbook as a legacy for our children and a gift for our readers. From our family to yours, we hope you take pleasure in making these recipes as much as we delight in sharing them with you.

mi mamá

I could write a whole book about *"mi mamá,"* but in the interest of space I will just share a few of my favorite stories. My sweetest memory of *mi mamá* is that she never turned a hungry soul away. I clearly remember a couple of times when strangers came to our door asking for food or a drink, because they had just crossed the border and had not eaten a thing in several days. She always gave them something. She taught me through example that no human being should ever be denied food, and especially something to drink. She was so very special that way.

Her desire to feed those she loved was most evident in her Sunday lunches. On Sundays after mass, her children and grandchildren would all make their rounds to visit her and food was always plentiful. It was like a family reunion every Sunday. My mother always had something delicious cooking on the stove or in the oven, and her welcoming words still ring in my ears, *"Siéntate a comer, esta muuuuy bueno."*

Maria de Jesus Mendias (Jesusita, as she was called) was born in the northern Mexican state of Julimes, Chihuahua. She came from a large family, nine girls and one boy who died at birth. She grew up on a cattle ranch and learned to cook at a young age alongside her mother and sisters. Together they spent hours cooking to feed their large family. Sometimes they even had unexpected guests, like soldiers of the Mexican revolution. At that time Pancho Villa's forces were based in Chihuahua, where Villa ruled over northern Mexico like a medieval warlord. Mamá would tell us some fascinating stories about Pancho Villa and his soldiers as they rode through their pueblo in Chihuahua, Mexico. The soldiers were infamous for raping young girls and so her protective parents were careful to hide their daughters in the barn. One day soldiers came to their home wanting more than a place to rest—they wanted the ranch itself! So her parents and sisters had no choice but to flee Mexico on a horse-drawn wagon with nothing but the clothes on their backs. The year was 1916 and my mother was only ten years old when they set forth to Ojinaga, Mexico, to cross the U.S. border into Texas. I know in my heart that difficult journey helped shape her into the courageous and independent woman she became.

Jesusita + Apolinar (sister)
1918

They eventually settled in El Rancho de Ochoa, where she met my father, Jose Soza. He was born and raised *en* La Haciendita. On December 27, 1924, she married my father in a small church in Shafter, Texas, which was a small mining town about sixty miles outside of Presidio, Texas. They lived in Presidio for a few years and had most of my siblings there and then they moved to Shafter, Texas. From 1939 to 1941 my parents owned Restaurante de Jesusita. My mother used to sell lunches to local miners. She was up prepping and cooking as early as 4 a.m. Her day began with *nixtamal*, the wet stone-ground tedious process for making dough for corn tortillas and tamales. The process of *nixtamalization* is as long as the name itself, its purpose to soften the hard walls of the corn kernels so they can be separated from the sweet, moist interior and then tossed away. Today there are *tortillerias*, tortilla bakeries that produce and sell fresh dough, but in those days it was a long process done by hand. *Nixtamal* required soaking *maize* (corn) overnight in an alkaline solution, usually limewater, and the next day rinsing, hulling, and grinding it. Every morning Mamá would hull the corn and kneel in front of a *metate* (mealing stone) to grind it, creating the dough for tortillas or tamales. Hominy (nixtamalized corn kernels) was also used for other dishes, like *pozole* (hominy stew) or *menudo* (hominy and tripe soup).

In 1941 my parents moved back to Presidio and in 1953 made their way to El Paso, Texas, where they bought a small home and built a grocery store adjacent to it, which they named Soza's Grocery. I was born in El Paso and am the youngest of nine children. While my mother worked in the grocery store, my father and my brother Carlos would buy produce from local warehouses and make bi-weekly trips in my father's pickup truck to Presidio selling the produce along the way. While in Presidio they bought the sweetest cantaloupes and watermelons and the spiciest chile peppers and then turned around and sold them to warehouses in El Paso and in our grocery store.

Jose + Jesusita
December 27, 1924

Apolonio + Friend + Jose

My father passed away in 1958, when he was only 53. I was ten years old; the same age my mother was when she crossed the border. I now look back and understand how quickly she had to grow up, because I too had to take on more responsibility as a ten year old. I helped her with the cooking and worked in the grocery store. At the age of 52 my mother was a widow, a single parent, and a business owner. She became our pillar of strength, and thankfully lived a long life until she passed at the age of 98.

Evangelina + Jesusita + Zavala & Curtis Grandchildren

I later purchased the family grocery store, which I owned and managed for 17 years. On the weekends I cooked and sold *menudo*, and during the week I sold burritos, *tortas* (Mexican sandwiches), and *cóctel de camarones* (Mexican shrimp cocktail). During the Lenten season I made and sold *capirotada* (Mexican bread pudding). In 2003, after 50 years in business and with no one else in the family to run it, I finally closed Soza's Grocery.

My love for food came from my mother, who made everything from scratch. She used to make her *salsa casera* (homemade salsa) with her bare hands before she owned a blender. She also made her red chile this way. She had such strong hands—I always wondered how her hands didn't burn from the peppers. I'll never forget her delicious tamales at Christmas and hearty *menudo* for New Years Day, or the taste of her fresh green chile *salsa casera* with homemade corn tortillas … mmm, it was the best.

You would always find my mother in the kitchen or in her garden. She loved to cook, bake, and tend to her little garden behind our home. She planted chiles, tomatoes, squash, corn, sugarcane, and fragrant herbs like cilantro, rosemary, and mint. We also had fruit trees—apple, peach, apricot, quince, and pomegranate. She made delicious *empanadas* and pies with the fruit from her trees. There were always wonderful aromas coming from her kitchen, like the smell of her freshly made flour tortillas, green chile roasting on the *comal* (iron griddle), and *frijoles de la olla* (beans from the pot) on the stove. And as she cooked, she would tell us wonderful stories of her childhood while living in Chihuahua and the mischief she would get into with her sisters.

SOZA'S groceries ~ est. 1953 ~

When my daughter Yvette asked me if I would work with her on this cookbook I was excited, but never imagined the work that lay before us. My oldest daughter Veronica also had dreams about gathering our family recipes and putting together a family cookbook. We soon decided that the best idea would be to collaborate and put all our memories and recipes into one book. It has brought the three of us so much closer together and for that I am forever grateful. With my daughters' Latin fusion recipes, my traditional south of the border home-style dishes, and my mother's old-world northern Mexican cuisine, we have a collection of recipes that make up the heart and soul of our homes. My son, Michael, has been a big inspiration and we couldn't have done this without his support. I am blessed to have such wonderful children.

Jesusita + Evangelina + Veronica + Yvette

I was fortunate to inherit my mother's love of *la cocina*. Cooking and baking is in my blood. Now when somebody comes into my kitchen, I can echo my mother's words, *"Siéntate a comer, esta muuuuy bueno."* Thank you, Mamá, for being an extraordinary mother and the most wonderful grandmother to my children. We love you, and all our beautiful memories of you will forever live in our hearts.

Evangelina

Jesusita
2002

finding my way back to the kitchen

 The first thing Mom taught me how to cook was an over-easy egg. It was a Saturday morning, a time she usually spent occupied with all the household chores. But she had promised that week to teach me how to cook an egg, and despite her busy morning I kept pestering her about it. My begging and persistence finally paid off—she knew I was not going to let it go so she dropped everything she was doing. After several failed attempts at turning my egg over without breaking the yolk, I finally got it right. Success! This would be the first of many "cooking lessons" from Mom. I was nine.

Years later while in junior high, though I continued to spend time there, my love for the kitchen had waned. I was a teenager and I didn't care much about cooking. I loved all the food Mom and Grandma made, but cooking seemed like a chore—too time-consuming—and the kitchen was not where I wanted to be. I preferred to be out with my friends. However, Mom insisted that I help with the prep work, aka grunt work. Prep work consisted of grating cheese, chopping vegetables, peeling potatoes, or dicing meat and I hated every minute of it. It wasn't until later, when I graduated from the prep work to making simple meals like tacos and quesadillas, and eventually trickier recipes like Mexican rice, that cooking became something I could learn to like, maybe.

My entire life I've been surrounded by marvelous food during every imaginable holiday and family get-together. Like most families, parties were an excuse for us to try new recipes and enjoy some oldies but goodies. Sunday lunch at my grandma's house meant perfectly prepared *caldo* (soup) or beef short ribs. Christmas Eve was not complete without tamales or *menudo* or both, and Fridays always guaranteed red enchiladas. Over the years my list of favorites continued to grow, but it wasn't until I left home after college that I found myself calling Mom and writing down the recipes. Eventually my pile of recipes grew and I referred to them as my pile of love.

While living overseas in Okinawa and later mainland Japan, I really started to think back to all the times I watched Grandma and Mom cooking and decided to try my hand at cooking more of our family's recipes utilizing my pile of love. My overseas friends enjoyed my efforts at making Mexican food and I was glad to have an audience so eager to taste all my experimenting. After all, anything was better than what was served at the one Mexican restaurant on Okinawa. I painstakingly tried to replicate things like *frijoles de la olla,* red and green enchiladas, and even *menudo*. After a while I became more confident in my cooking and I wasn't afraid of making mistakes. I relied heavily on my pile of love, my memory, and brief tips from Mom over the telephone. Sometimes she'd mail me handwritten recipes, which I treasured—almost twenty years later, I still have some of them.

I decided years ago that I'd write a cookbook, a compilation of all my favorite recipes as the ultimate pile of love. Instead of going at it alone I am fortunate enough to be writing with my sister Yvette and our beautiful Mom. This cookbook is a little bit of me and a lot about those stories and recipes I hold dear in my heart. I began this journey as a means of preserving my past for my children, and over the years it has become a tasty timeline of anecdotes and stories I had almost forgotten. So this book is to honor Mom and Grandma, who have given me a passion for cooking. Grandma, you're right, food does nourish the soul. And to our readers—may you find refuge in the kitchen and learn to love it as much as I have.

Veronica

Veronica + Jesusita

a memory

I vividly remember kneeling for hours on a chair in Grandma's cozy *cocina* listening to her childhood stories and watching her cook. I loved hearing about her family's journey from Mexico to Presidio and finally to El Paso, Texas. My favorite stories were of the times her mother and sisters had to cook for soldiers of the Mexican revolution at their ranch in Chihuahua, Mexico.

I can still picture her cheerful kitchen in El Paso as if it were only yesterday. It had curtains that my mother made for her and two parakeets—one green, the other yellow—chirping in their cage and keeping Grandma company. The parakeets always seemed so happy, especially when Grandma had her radio on and she sang in the kitchen. It's as if they were singing along with her. If I close my eyes, I can still hear the parakeets and smell green chiles roasting and fresh flour tortillas cooking on her *comal* (iron griddle). Just thinking about the tortillas and green chiles makes my mouth water. I spent a lot of time in Grandma's kitchen while Mom was at work, and it was like home to me.

Grandma made flour tortillas almost every day and fresh salsa when needed. I was mesmerized as she would knead the dough, form perfect little balls, roll them out with her small wooden rolling pin, and then cook the tortillas on a *comal*. I'd sit and wait patiently and loved watching a tall pile of fresh tortillas accumulate. One of my favorite parts was when the tortilla would rise and she would press down on the trapped air inside it, creating a hissing sound. I can still see her doing this with a rolled up *limpiador* (dish cloth) in her hand. I always looked forward to eating the first warm tortilla spread with butter or fresh salsa.

After making the tortillas she would make some *salsa casera*. First she'd roast the long green chiles, and then she'd peel them. Instead of using a blender, she would squeeze the roasted chiles and tomatoes with her bare hands to make the salsa. Just being near the chiles made my eyes water, but her hands seemed magically impervious to the burn. From my child's perspective, her hands looked so strong and yet so gentle to me. As I watched her make the salsa, she'd tell me stories about how she picked cotton as a little girl and washed clothes by hand using a metal washboard in boiling water. It was then I realized why her hands looked so strong—she had labored with them her entire life to feed and clothe her family.

Jesusita + Yvette

As I knelt on that chair, I absorbed every word, every sigh, every bit of passion and wisdom from her stories. My grandmother always counseled me when I needed it the most. I remember her telling me not to compare myself to others, which has always been a challenge for me. She always reminded me to be happy with everything I had and not to take anything for granted. When she passed away, my Mom asked me if I wanted something that reminded me of Grandma. I remember thinking, all I want is one of the two rolling pins she used to make her legendary flour tortillas. I called my Mom a few weeks after Grandma's passing and asked if anyone had asked for them. It turned out my sister had asked for one of her rolling pins too and my Uncle Carlos had the other one. However, he was more than happy to give it to me. I took that as a sign that her rolling pin was meant to be mine. It's that beautiful, old wooden rolling pin that sits prominently on my kitchen counter today—that same rolling pin that sparked the idea to gather our family's recipes and stories for my children.

Grandma's rolling pin continues to inspire me to cook and write down recipes handed down from my mother and Grandma, and encourages me to create some of my own recipes, which are also in this cookbook. Writing this cookbook with both my mother and sister has been a journey back in time—the sweet memories of my childhood, our family gatherings, and the simple and happy life we all shared.

Yvette

glossary of chiles

The chile is a versatile fruit that comes in a wide variety of shapes, colors, sizes, and hotness. It can be prepared in a myriad of ways: roasted (our favorite), fried, boiled, grilled, and/or fresh. In this glossary we focus on our favorite chiles.

All the chiles in this glossary are used throughout this cookbook to create a variety of salsas and sauces to compliment a recipe or as the main ingredient in a recipe. We use roasted green chiles and red chile sauce for several of our recipes. Following the glossary are the steps for how to prepare the two.

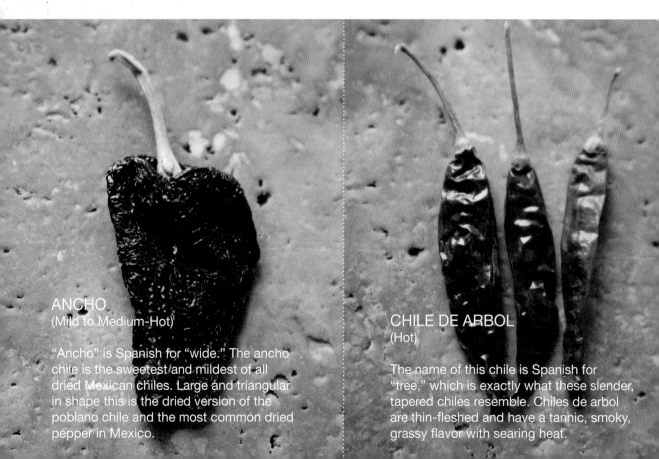

ANCHO
(Mild to Medium-Hot)

"Ancho" is Spanish for "wide." The ancho chile is the sweetest and mildest of all dried Mexican chiles. Large and triangular in shape this is the dried version of the poblano chile and the most common dried pepper in Mexico.

CHILE DE ARBOL
(Hot)

The name of this chile is Spanish for "tree," which is exactly what these slender, tapered chiles resemble. Chiles de arbol are thin-fleshed and have a tannic, smoky, grassy flavor with searing heat.

CHILE GÜERO
(Medium)

These chiles are called güeros (blondies) in Mexico because of their yellow color. They have a mild flavor.

PASILLA
(Medium to Hot)

The word "pasilla" comes from the word "pasa" which means "little black raisin." This thin-fleshed chile has a berry flavor with aromatic overtones.

CHIPOTLE
(Hot)

This is actually a dried, smoked, red jalapeño. You'll know it by its light-brown color and smoky scent with hints of chocolate and tobacco.

DRIED RED CHILE
(Mild to Hot)

Also referred to as chile colorado, New Mexico chile, or California chile, this chile has a thin flesh with an earthy chile flavor and undertones of wild cherries. This is the chile we use to make our Red Chile Sauce.

ROASTING CHILE PEPPERS

Preheat broiler.

Select firm, meaty peppers without wrinkles. Rinse thoroughly to remove dust particles.

Place peppers evenly in a single layer on a foil-lined cookie sheet. Pierce each chile with a knife.

Place under broiler. Watch them closely as the skin will blister and turn black within minutes. Turn the peppers after 3 to 5 minutes to blister all sides evenly. When done, the pepper skins should be evenly blistered and mostly black.

Place roasted peppers in a plastic bag, cover with a wet kitchen towel and when cool, peel off blackened skin. Tear open and pull out the seed pod and stem unless you are making chile rellenos. In which case you will simply remove the stem carefully along with the seeds, leaving the chile intact for stuffing.

ANAHEIM
(Mild to Medium)

Anaheim chiles are perfect for recipes calling for roasted chiles to make salsas or chile rellenos. The riper dried, red form of this chile is called chile colorado.

JALAPEÑO
(Medium to Hot)

Jalapeños have the richest flavor of all the small chiles, which makes them perfect for salsas.

POBLANO
(Mild to Medium)

This heart-shaped chile—wider and darker than an Anaheim—is also mild. It has a wide interior which makes it the perfect chile for stuffing.

SERRANO
(Hot)

The flavor of serrano chiles is bright and biting with a delayed fuse. These small, skinny, pointy chiles are about five times hotter than jalapeños.

red chile sauce

We didn't have a lot of money growing up, so nothing was wasted. I remember eating red chile for days. For example, if Mom or Grandma made red sauce for enchiladas one day, the leftover red chile would be used to make *chile colorado con carne* the next day, and then the following day, the leftover *chile colorado con carne* would be poured on top of little corn tartlets called *sopes*. On other occasions if there was leftover red chile sauce, Mom would make us *chilaquiles* for breakfast. We ate this stuff all the time. As a kid I'd protest because I just didn't get it. "I love red enchiladas, but I just don't understand why we have to eat the red sauce with so many other dishes." My complaint went unacknowledged and so the routines continued. It wasn't until I left home that I went through what could only be called a fierce chile withdrawal. Suddenly I craved all the recipes made with red chile sauce.

Grandma always had red enchiladas on Fridays. I think Enchilada Fridays started during Lent, a Catholic observance that partially focuses on charity and doing without luxuries. As a part of this, no meat is consumed on Fridays from Ash Wednesday until Easter. I'm so glad this Lenten tradition lived on all year long in our home. I loved the intoxicating aroma coming from Grandma's house next door when she made the red chile sauce. As soon as she started frying the sauce I knew it was almost time to eat. If I was in the kitchen she'd let me help by grating the Colby cheese to go with the enchiladas.

Family and friends would always come over on Fridays to have Grandma's red enchiladas. Cousins, aunts, uncles, second cousins, you name it, they came over. I'd try to linger nearby and listen to some of the *chismes* (gossip) and *historias* (stories), but was never allowed to hang out long enough to hear all the juicy details. As soon as the conversation got interesting I was told to go outside and play. I didn't stay out for long; as soon as someone else arrived at Grandma's house, I was back in the kitchen.

Grandma always made one large black cast iron pot of red chile sauce and it would feed everyone who showed up. I remember staring into the pot after a group of aunts or cousins would leave, dumbfounded by the fact that the pot was still filled with sauce. It's not easy to whip up another batch of red enchilada sauce from scratch, so I knew Grandma didn't do that. I never saw Grandma refill it so I decided early on that it was a magical pot, a pot that would refill itself just because she loved everyone enough to feed the masses. The next group of hungry family members would walk through her doors and eat a stack of red enchiladas, leaving just in time to give Grandma a short break before the next group arrived.

The enchiladas I grew up eating were not rolled and filled with meat or cheese inside; they were better—stacked (*montadas*) like pancakes. Each tortilla was fried softly in hot oil, then dipped into the red sauce, placed flat on a plate and then sprinkled with cheese and finely chopped onions. We usually ate about 3 to 4 enchiladas *montadas* along with a side of *frijoles de la olla* and *sopa de arroz*. If you were adventuresome enough, you would request a fried egg over-easy, which sat on top of this heap of goodness. As a kid I liked watching the yolk run down the sides of my enchiladas; as an adult I think it's just criminal to let it get that far. If the yolk does meet the plate, I quickly scoop it up with a forkful of enchilada.

This would all start about noon on Friday and go into the dinner hours. Latecomers would drag themselves in after a long day at work, hoping to find some sauce left, only to be disappointed to see the sauce starting to dry at the bottom of the pot.

Making the sauce from scratch takes a while, but once it's made, it refrigerates and freezes well for other recipes in this cookbook. This is the same sauce used to make tamales and our family's *menudo* recipe.

RED CHILE SAUCE
CHILE COLORADO

I remember *mi mamá* standing at her kitchen table squeezing the boiled red chile pods with her bare hands; this was before she owned a blender. I never quite figured out how she did this because the chiles were extremely spicy, but her hands never seemed to feel the burn. Afterwards she would strain the red chiles by turning a wooden pestle around and around in a conical strainer and pressing down on the chile pods. This would result in the velvety rich chile that she used for so many recipes.

8 ounces California or New Mexico red chile pods

6 cups water

6 tablespoons all-purpose flour

4 cloves garlic

1 tablespoon salt

Remove stems, seeds, and veins from the chile pods. Place in a colander and rinse well with cool water.

Add the chiles to a large pot and add enough water so they are just covered. Bring water to a boil. Lower the heat, cover, and simmer for about 20 minutes. After 10 minutes turn the chiles over with tongs to make sure the chiles soften evenly. Drain cooked pods and allow time to cool down before blending. Discard water.

Fill blender with 3 cups of water, half of the cooled chile pods, 3 tablespoons flour, 2 cloves garlic, and half of the salt. Blend until smooth. Strain sauce through a fine sieve to remove skins and seeds; discard skins and seeds. Repeat blending and straining process with remaining water, pods, flour, garlic, and salt. If necessary, season with more salt.

This sauce can be made in advance and kept in airtight containers in the refrigerator or freezer. Red chile sauce can be stored in the refrigerator for up to one week or frozen for up to six months.

MAKES 6 TO 7 CUPS

tamales

 *Mi mamá* made these delicious tamales every year for our family gatherings on Christmas Eve. Everybody loved her tamales; she made them with so much love, it was her Christmas gift to her *familia*. She would always say, "You have to make them with a lot of filling, or you will be eating just *masa*." She didn't own a large mixer, so she always prepared the *masa* by hand. I'm not sure she would have used a mixer even if she had owned one. There was something about the effort put into mixing it by hand that made them all the more delicious.

Christmas was one holiday that I always waited for with great anticipation. I cherish the times that I spent in the kitchen with *mi mamá*, I learned to make her wonderful tamales and it was a time to talk about so many things. She would tell me stories of when she was young, when she met and married my father, and their life in Presidio, Texas. They were stories that I loved listening to, it didn't matter how many times I heard them. Then when my children were old enough to help, they were there to rinse the corn husks and to listen to her singing while she worked. She always had her radio playing old Mexican songs, and if she didn't have the radio on she would sing church hymns or her favorite folk song, *"De Colores."* Those are times that I will never forget, the precious mother, grandmother, and great-grandmother that she was.

TAMALE DOUGH
TAMALE MASA

The most vital ingredient in making the perfect tamal is the *masa*. *Masa* is the plain, wet stone-ground dough made with a special corn known as *nixtamal*. Fresh *masa* can be purchased in one of two ways, prepared and unprepared. Our family prefers to purchase unprepared *masa* and then we add lard, salt, broth, and baking powder, giving it the *muy bueno* touch. So if you choose to use our recipe make sure you purchase *sin preparar* (unprepared *masa*). Grandma prepared it this way for years and so do we. *Masa* can be purchased in Mexican specialty stores.

2 pounds lard (see Note)

2 teaspoons baking powder, divided

2 tablespoons salt, divided

5 pounds fresh ground masa (unprepared) for tamales, divided

2 to 3 cups broth from cooked pork roast (page 34) or chicken broth, divided

½ cup Red Chile Sauce (page 25; only add if making red chile pork tamales)

MAKE TAMALE MASA:
Place 1 pound of lard in a large stand mixer and mix until fluffy, scraping sides so the lard stays in the center of the mixing bowl. (The flat beater is the ideal accessory for mixing.) Add half the baking powder and half the salt to the lard and mix together.

Add half the masa and mix together. Slowly add half the broth and half the red chile sauce, if using, to the masa and mix until combined. The mixture should be about the consistency of smooth peanut butter. If not, add more broth as necessary. Test the masa by taking a small piece (½ teaspoon) and dropping it into a cup of warm water. If it floats it is ready; if it sinks, add a little more lard, beat for another minute and test it again. Repeat this process until the masa floats. Pour the masa mixture into a bigger bowl. Repeat the process with the remaining ingredients.

Cover the masa and set aside while you prepare your filling of choice (see pages 34-37).

(CONTINUED)

Note: If you are using rendered lard you will need to use less broth.

ASSEMBLE TAMALES

PREPARE OJAS (CORN HUSKS):

Soak corn husks in water for an hour before using, rinse well with running water to take off any dust or corn husk fibers. To keep corn husks pliable and easy to work with, keep in water while filling tamales. Place a handful of wet corn husks in a colander to drain before using.

SPREAD MASA:

Place the wide end of the husk on the palm of your hand, narrow end is at the top. Starting at the middle of the husk spread 2 tablespoons of the masa with the back of a spoon in a rectangle or oval shape, using a downward motion towards the wide-bottom edge. Do not spread the masa to the ends; leave about a 2-inch border on the left and right sides of the husk.

FILL CORN HUSKS:

Spoon 1½ tablespoons of your chosen filling down the center of the masa. Fold both sides to the center; finish off by bringing the pointed end of the husk toward the filled end. Make sure it's a snug closure so the tamal will not open during steaming. Secure by tying a thin strip of corn husk around the tamal. This will keep the tamal from unwrapping during the steaming process, especially if the husk is too thick and will not stay folded.

STEAM TAMALES:

Use a deep pot or tamale steamer to steam tamales. If using a tamale steamer fill with water up to the fill line. Set the tamale rack over the water. Place tamales upright, with fold against the sides of the other tamales to keep them from unfolding. Cover pot with a tightly fitting lid. Set heat on high and bring to a boil, about 15 minutes. Lower heat and simmer for 2½ to 3 hours. Keep lid on tightly. To test if done, put one tamal on a plate and take off the corn husk. If it comes off without sticking to the tamal they are done.

MAKES 6 TO 7 DOZEN TAMALES

RED CHILE AND PORK TAMALES
TAMALES DE PUERCO CON CHILE COLORADO

SHREDDED PORK

7 to 8 pounds pork butt or pork shoulder

2½ cups water

1 tablespoon sea salt

FILLING

6 tablespoons broth with fat pieces from
   cooked pork

3 tablespoons all-purpose flour

6½ cups Red Chile Sauce (page 25)

1 tablespoon salt

1 batch tamale masa (page 31)

Corn husks (ojas)

MAKE PORK:

Place pork, water, and salt in a slow cooker
and cook for 6 to 8 hours. After meat is
cooked, remove from the slow cooker and
let cool to room temperature. Shred pork and
remove fat while shredding, reserving fat.
(Usually, after pork is cooked and shredded,
you will be left with about 3 pounds of meat.)

In a blender combine the cooled broth from the
cooked pork and the leftover fat pieces. Blend
and reserve for using when making tamale
masa and filling. Broth can be kept, tightly
covered, for 1 week in the refrigerator. The
broth also freezes well and will keep for 4 to 6
months.

MAKE FILLING:

Heat the 6 tablespoons broth in a large skillet.
Add flour and whisk for at least 4 to 5 minutes.

Add red chile sauce and salt, stir, and cook for
10 minutes. The chile sauce will be very thick
at this time.

Add the 3 pounds shredded pork and stir so all
the pork is well coated with the red chile sauce.
Simmer for at least 10 minutes. Let mixture
cool before filling tamales (see directions on
page 32).

FILLS ABOUT 5 DOZEN TAMALES

GREEN CHILE AND PORK TAMALES
TAMALES DE PUERCO CON CHILE VERDE

2 tablespoons olive oil

3 tablespoons all-purpose flour

5 cups diced, roasted and peeled Anaheim
chiles (see page 20)

2 teaspoons garlic powder

Salt to taste

2½ pounds cooked shredded pork (page 34)

¼ to ½ cup chicken broth

1 batch tamale masa (page 31)

Corn husks (ojas)

Heat oil in a heavy skillet or deep pot. Add flour
and whisk for 3 minutes to prevent clumping.

Add diced green chiles and cook for 3 minutes,
stirring so mixture doesn't stick to the skillet. Let
come to a boil. Lower heat; add garlic powder
and salt to taste.

Add pork and broth and let come to a boil and
simmer for 5 minutes, allowing flavors to come
together. Let mixture cool before filling tamales
(see directions on page 32).

FILLS ABOUT 5 DOZEN TAMALES

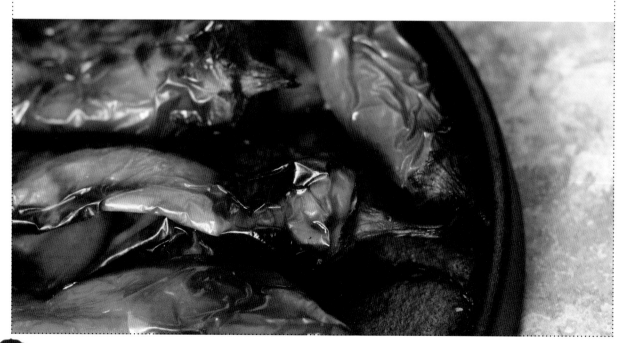

CHEESE WITH ROASTED CHILE TAMALES

TAMALES DE QUESO CON RAJAS

2 tablespoons olive oil

3 tablespoons all-purpose flour

5 cups diced, roasted and peeled Anaheim chiles (see page 20)

1 tablespoon garlic powder

½ cup suero (whey) or buttermilk

1½ teaspoons salt

4½ cups shredded asadero, quesadilla, or Muenster cheese, divided

1 batch tamale masa (page 31)

Corn husks (ojas)

Heat olive oil, add flour and stir for 3 minutes. Add diced green chiles and garlic powder and stir for 5 minutes.

Add suero, salt, and ½ cup of shredded cheese, and simmer for 7 minutes, stirring until cheese melts and mixture thickens. Reserve the additional shredded cheese to sprinkle over mixture in each tamal (about 1 tablespoon each). Let mixture cool before filling tamales (see directions page 32).

FILLS ABOUT 5 DOZEN TAMALES

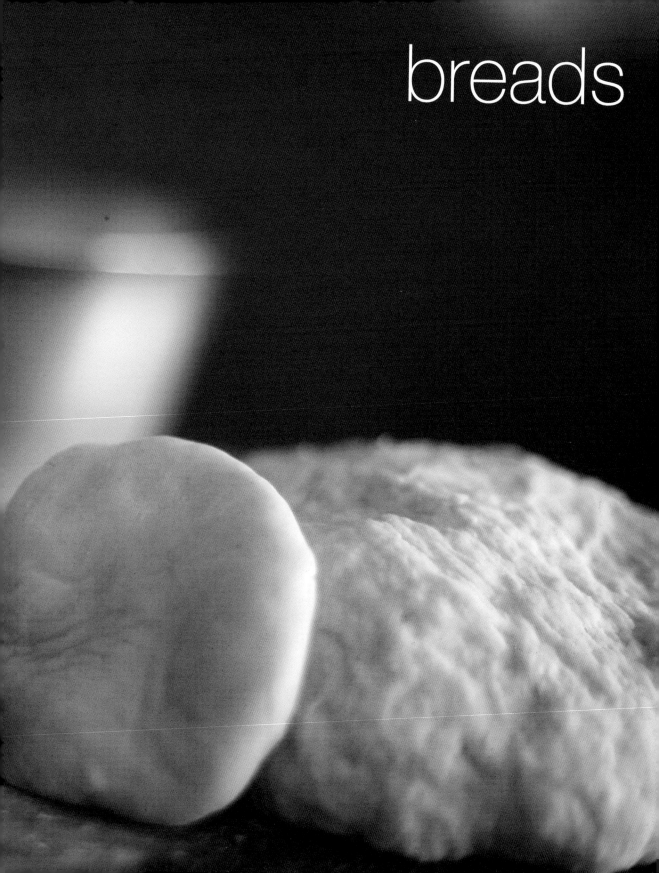

breads

HOMEMADE CORN TORTILLAS
TORTILLAS DE MAIZ

 I have not mastered all of my mother's old-world recipes, but I keep at it, attempting to capture the essence of each one. Homemade corn tortillas are the perfect example. I don't think I will ever be able to make them like *mi mamá*. But it doesn't mean I won't keep trying.

Mi mamá never used a tortilla press when making corn tortillas. She would place a bowl of water on the table. Then she would wet her fingers with water from the bowl and scoop up some *masa*, and clap the dough ball back and forth between her hands until it was a flat tortilla (but not too thin). She would then cook the tortilla on the warm *comal* and repeated this cycle until all of the *masa* was used.

But *mi mamá* also taught me a simpler way. She would make a small ball of *masa*, put it on a cotton dishcloth, fold the cloth over the ball and press down on it with a dinner plate. Out came a perfectly round tortilla.

Today there is a much easier way to make corn tortillas using a tortilla press. That's how my girls make their homemade tortillas. For those of us who want to do it the old-fashioned way, please keep trying.

(CONTINUED)

HOMEMADE CORN TORTILLAS
(CONTINUED)

2 cups masa harina (corn flour)

½ teaspoon salt

1⅛ cups water

Place a comal (griddle or cast-iron skillet) over medium heat and allow it to heat up.

In a large mixing bowl mix flour, salt, and water for about 4 minutes. If the masa (dough) doesn't come together well add 1 tablespoon of water at a time and mix some more.

Divide the masa into 16 dough balls and press down slightly on each one. Keep the masa covered with a dishtowel so it does not dry out while you press the tortillas.

Use a tortilla press when making corn tortillas. Place a piece of plastic wrap over each end of the tortilla press. The ball of masa will sit between the two pieces of plastic wrap during the pressing process. Place a ball of masa on one end of the tortilla press, directly on the plastic wrap. Close the tortilla press and press down on the handle, flattening the masa and creating a corn tortilla. Open the press and you should have a corn tortilla beautifully pressed.

Place the corn tortilla on the hot comal to cook for approximately 30 seconds, or until browned and slightly puffy. Turn tortilla over to brown on second side for approximately 30 seconds more, and then transfer to a tortilla warmer or basket lined with a dish towel. This is how Grandma stored hers. Continue making tortillas with the remaining masa balls.

MAKES 16 TORTILLAS

HOMEMADE FLOUR TORTILLAS
TORTILLAS DE HARINA

 Every other day Grandma used to make her famous homemade flour tortillas. As soon as I entered Grandma's kitchen, I could smell that special aroma that only comes from freshly made tortillas. If you've ever had the luxury of being in a kitchen when tortillas are cooking on the *comal* (cast iron skillet), you know what I'm talking about. I remember rubbing a stick of butter on my warm tortilla and watching the butter melt. I'd quickly roll the tortilla and eat it; sometimes the butter would run down my arm which was okay because I would just lick it right off.

 I remember running to Grandma's house after school knowing that she would be rolling and cooking tortillas. She would give me a small ball of dough and I'd roll out my own tortilla. Mine was always shaped like an oval, never perfectly round like Grandma's. My favorite way to eat a fresh warm tortilla is with a dollop of *salsa casera* (page 60), lightly salted, and rolled into one perfect spicy burrito.

(CONTINUED)

HOMEMADE FLOUR TORTILLAS
(CONTINUED)

4 cups all-purpose flour

¾ teaspoon baking powder

1⅛ teaspoons salt

1 tablespoon lard or shortening

1¼ cups warm water

Place a comal (griddle or cast-iron skillet) over medium heat and allow it to heat up.

In a bowl combine all the dry ingredients. Add the lard or shortening and combine until you have the consistency of small crumbs.

Add the warm water and mix well with your hand. The mixture may be a little sticky. Knead on a cutting board or smooth counter until dough is pliable and springy. Sprinkle with flour if dough is too sticky.

Form 2 to 2½-inch dough balls. With a rolling pin, roll out the dough balls to form 7 to 8-inch disks. If dough is sticky, sprinkle board and rolling pin with flour to make it easier to roll out the dough.

As you roll out each disk, place on the hot comal to cook, it will take 1 minute or less on each side. After cooking the first side, turn tortilla over and let it cook on the opposite side; when tortilla starts to form air pockets press down gently on it with a wooden tortilla press or rolled up kitchen towel (like Grandma did) to release the air. Don't press too much, or it will make tough tortillas.

Keep the tortillas warm in a tortilla warmer or under a clean dish towel while you make the rest. Leftover tortillas can be refrigerated in a plastic bag.

MAKES 13 TO 14 (7 TO 8 INCH) TORTILLAS

BUTTERMILK BISCUITS
GALLETAS DE SUERO

These biscuits or *galletas* have been made by Mom as far back as I can remember. They are best warm and fresh out of the oven. I take one, split it in half, and while it's still warm put a big clump of butter on it and watch it melt. If it's more of a meal I want, I just add some refried beans, a slice of *queso,* and some *salsita,* and then put the other half on top and eat it while it's hot. Or you can add a few slices of avocado and sprinkle with a little salt. *Sabroso*!

4 cups all-purpose flour

1½ teaspoons baking powder

⅓ cup shortening

2 cups suero (whey) or buttermilk

Preheat oven to 350 degrees F.

In a large mixing bowl combine flour and baking powder. Cut in shortening until well mixed. Make a well in center of mixture and slowly add suero. Knead dough with your fingers until smooth and add additional suero when necessary. It's all right if the dough is sticky, more flour can be added. But I like it a little bit sticky—the galletas come out flakier.

Divide dough into 12 to 14 balls. Pat each ball out until about 1-inch thick. Place on ungreased cookie sheet and poke each galleta with a fork twice. Bake for 20 to 23 minutes.

Set the oven to broil and broil for 1 additional minute or until golden brown.

MAKES 1 DOZEN BISCUITS

Note: Every oven differs so watch these carefully the last 5 minutes to make sure not to over bake or, dare I say it, burn them.

salsas

AVOCADO AND TOMATILLO SALSA
SALSA DE AGUACATE Y TOMATILLO

A warning—this salsa can be addictive! I first tasted it in Ixtapa, Mexico, and I just had to figure out how to make it myself at home. Fortunately it is actually a very simple salsa, and tastes so great with a bowl of tortilla chips and a nice cold beer on a sunny day. The creaminess of the avocados combined with the pop of spice from jalapeños and serranos make this salsa irresistible. Use this salsa to top tacos, *gorditas* (page 178), or *sopes* (page 168).

8 tomatillos, husks removed, rinsed

1 or 2 serrano peppers, stemmed

2 jalapeño peppers, stemmed

1 unpeeled clove garlic

3 avocados, pitted and peeled

Handful cilantro

2 cups water

1 teaspoon salt

Preheat oven to broil. Roast the tomatillos, serrano peppers, jalapeños peppers, and garlic on a foil-lined baking sheet until blackened all over, about 5 minutes. Flip them over and roast the other sides for an additional 4 to 5 minutes. Watch carefully to prevent the tomatillos from burning.

Place roasted peppers in a plastic bag, close the bag and allow the peppers to steam until the skins loosen, about 10 minutes.

While the peppers are cooling off, peel off skin from garlic and discard. After the peppers have steamed, peel skin off and discard.

Place in a blender the cooled tomatillos, roasted and peeled peppers, roasted garlic, avocados, cilantro, water, and salt. Blend until creamy.

MAKES 3½ TO 4 CUPS

CHOPPED TOMATO SALSA
PICO DE GALLO

I call this *la bandera* (flag) salsa because it has the three colors of the Mexican flag: green, white, and red. This happens to be the salsa that I notice at almost all salsa bars in both restaurants and fast food *taquerias*. Your salsa will taste the best if you use fresh ingredients during their peak season, summer and fall. The longer the salsa sits the tomatoes start releasing their own juices and make the salsa too watery, so Mom came up with the idea of adding tomato sauce; it helps the salsa thicken without losing its tomato flavor or overpowering the other ingredients.

1 jalapeño pepper, stemmed and chopped

1 serrano pepper, stemmed and chopped

3 small Roma or vine-ripened tomatoes, chopped

1 small white onion, chopped

1 tablespoon chopped cilantro

½ teaspoon salt

Juice of 1 lime

¼ cup tomato sauce

Put chopped jalapeño, serrano, tomatoes, onion, and cilantro in a large mixing bowl and sprinkle with salt.

Add lime juice and tomato sauce. Mix well and taste and add additional salt if necessary.

Serve as a topping on fish, chicken, grilled steak, or with a basket of tortilla chips.

MAKES 2 CUPS

MANGO AND AVOCADO SALSA
SALSA DE AGUACATE Y MANGO

 In our home we love all things mango: mango ice cream, sorbet, smoothies, margaritas, *paletas*, salsas, you name it, we've made it. Here is a cheerful salsa made with two of our favorite tropical fruits, mangos and avocados. Spoon it over pan-fried tilapia (page 195) or just set it out as a side dish and watch it disappear.

1 large ripe mango, peeled, pitted, and chopped

1 small red onion, finely chopped

1 avocado, pitted, peeled, and chopped

2 roma tomatoes, peeled, seeded, and chopped

3 tablespoons chopped fresh cilantro

1 serrano pepper, finely chopped

3 tablespoons lime juice

1 teaspoon olive oil

Salt to taste

Combine the chopped mango, red onion, avocado, tomatoes, cilantro, and serrano pepper in a bowl. Add the lime juice and olive oil and toss gently. Add salt to taste. Set aside and let all the flavors come together at room temperature.

MAKES 2 TO 2½ CUPS

MUSHROOM, JALAPEÑO, AND CILANTRO SALSA
SALSA DE HONGOS Y JALAPEÑOS

Mushroom salsa? Believe it or not, it's a nice change from the usual tomato-based variety. If you love mushrooms like me, you're probably drooling over the idea of mushrooms as the main ingredient in a salsa. Actually it's not mushrooms *in* the salsa, mushrooms *are* the salsa. The addition of lime juice softens the texture of the mushrooms the longer they marinate, allowing the jalapeño and cilantro to work their magic on the mushrooms and blend all the flavors into one darn good salsa. For those of you not crazy about mushrooms, never say never, until you've tried this salsa.

1 pound fresh white mushrooms, finely chopped

1 small red onion, finely chopped

2 jalapeño peppers, stemmed and finely chopped

Handful cilantro, chopped

¾ cup fresh lime juice

1 tablespoon olive oil

Salt to taste

In a bowl combine the mushrooms, onion, jalapeño, and cilantro. Add the lime juice and olive oil and toss gently. Salt to taste.

Let sit for a couple of hours allowing the flavors to meld. This salsa is best served at room temperature.

Serve as a topping for fish, chicken, grilled steak, or as an appetizer with a basket of your favorite tortilla chips.

MAKES 3 CUPS

TOMATILLO SALSA
SALSA VERDE

I love hot and spicy salsas but my husband doesn't, so this salsa is for him and those like him who prefer salsa without too much heat. Tomatillos are not something we grew up eating. I know, I know, but we have them now and they are magnificent to cook with. What I like most about this salsa is the tanginess of the tomatillos. The combination of the tomatillos with the roasted garlic, chile peppers, onions, and cilantro gives this salsa a lot of punch without a lot of heat. You can serve *salsa verde* with homemade *tostadas*, a warm *queso fresco*, or simply spooned over eggs in the morning.

8 tomatillos, husks removed and rinsed

2 unpeeled cloves garlic

2 serrano peppers, stemmed and coarsely chopped

1 jalapeño pepper, stemmed and coarsely chopped

¼ yellow onion, chopped

Handful cilantro

½ teaspoon salt

Boil tomatillos in water to cover for about 15 minutes. Remove tomatillos from the water and allow them to cool before blending.

Roast the garlic cloves in their skins in a dry pan until skin is charred, about 10 minutes. Cool and remove skins.

In a blender place the cooled tomatillos, roasted garlic, chopped serrano and jalapeño peppers, onion, cilantro, and salt and blend for about 1 minute. Do not over blend. Salsa should be chunky. Taste and add more salt if needed.

MAKES 2 TO 3 CUPS

JESUSITA'S HOUSE SALSA
SALSA CASERA DE JESUSITA

 This is the salsa *mi mamá* would make with her bare hands. I can't imagine how squeezing the roasted chiles with her bare hands didn't burn them, truly something amazing. I loved her *salsa casera* so much I would make salsa burritos, one right after the other, until she'd make me stop. She was afraid I would eat it all and not leave any for the rest of the family or get a stomachache. Luckily I must have inherited her cast-iron stomach, because I never got a stomachache from eating too much salsa or spicy chile!

6 to 7 Anaheim chiles, roasted and peeled (see page 20)

1 or 2 jalapeño peppers, roasted (optional)

½ teaspoon salt

3 cloves garlic, finely diced

1 (14.5-ounce) can whole tomato

¼ cup tomato sauce

In a food processor or blender, pulse the roasted and peeled chiles, jalapeño peppers, if using, salt, garlic, canned tomatoes, and tomato sauce for a few seconds. You do not want to puree it—chunky is best with this flavorful salsa.

This salsa is a perfect appetizer with a basket of your favorite tortilla chips or as the base for several of our recipes.

MAKES 3 CUPS

CHILE DE ARBOL SALSA
SALSA DE CHILE DE ARBOL

The smoky flavor of this salsa pairs well with beef, and Mom always serves it alongside her brisket (page 155). In fact, I can always count on finding this salsa in Mom's refrigerator. She and I like very spicy salsas, and we love the intensity of this one. Grandma always had a mild *salsa casera* (page 60) in her kitchen and Mom always has a smoky and spicy chile de arbol salsa in hers. I have to confess that Mom and I have eaten an entire bowl of this salsa with a bag of chips in one sitting on more than one occasion. My brother (who is not fond of spicy chiles) once watched in horror as Mom and I managed to do this.

1 teaspoon canola oil

20 chiles de arbol, stemmed (do not remove seeds or veins)

1 small white onion, chopped

2 cloves garlic, crushed

1 cup canned peeled whole tomatoes

1 (8-ounce) can tomato sauce

1 teaspoon salt

Heat canola oil in a medium skillet over medium heat. Add chiles and toast for 1 to 2 minutes, stirring constantly so chiles are fried well and change color.

Add onion and garlic and fry for 2 minutes, again stirring constantly.

Transfer fried ingredients to a food processor or blender and add whole tomatoes, tomato sauce, and salt. Puree until salsa is smooth with specks of chiles. Add salt to taste.

Serve at room temperature or slightly chilled. Serve as a salsa dip or to top off your favorite tacos or tostadas. Chile de arbol salsa can be stored in the refrigerator 3 to 5 days, or frozen for many weeks.

MAKES 2½ CUPS

drinks

BLOOD ORANGE MEZCAL MARGARITA

Mezcal and blood red oranges—a match made in a cocktail shaker! If you enjoy tequila as much as I do (and I do) then giving mezcal a try is well worth the experience. Mezcal is not the tequila of days gone by, with the scary worm at the bottom of the bottle. Mezcal has come a long way and the varieties available today are so worthy of the blood red oranges. If you don't have mezcal or just want to stick with what you know, then añejo tequila is what you want to use as it has some similar deep and dark notes like mezcal. Squeeze, pour, shake, pour again, and sip … ahhh. *Salud!*

Juice of 3 blood oranges

Juice of 3 cara cara oranges (also called red navel)

Juice of 3 limes

4 ounces Mezcal tequila

2 tablespoons simple syrup (page 105)

Ice

Salt for glass rims

Put the freshly squeezed juices in a martini shaker. Add the tequila, simple syrup, and ice. Shake and divide equally between two salt-rimmed margarita glasses. Garnish with a blood orange slice or a sprig of mint.

MAKES 2 MARGARITAS

CRANBERRY MARGARITA

Hola, tequila, meet the luscious, gorgeous, ruby-red cranberry. Together these two make a mouth-watering holiday drink that'll dazzle your taste buds. Cranberries aren't just for Thanksgiving anymore, now you can enjoy this tart berry with a little Grand Marnier, tequila, and freshly squeezed orange juice. I love cranberries, so it was only a matter of time before I concocted a drink marrying cranberries and tequila. The crystallized swizzle stick gives it an extra little sparkle to impress your guests.

1 cup granulated sugar

Juice of 4 oranges

1 (16-ounce) package fresh cranberries

15 ounces of your favorite silver tequila

5 ounces Grand Marnier

CRANBERRY SWIZZLE STICKS

1 (16-ounce) package cranberries

10 bamboo skewers

½ cup light corn syrup (recommend Karo Light)

⅓ cup water

1 cup granulated sugar

In a saucepan over medium heat, melt the sugar in the orange juice. Add the cranberries and cook over low heat for 10 minutes. Set cranberry mixture aside and let cool. Blend in a blender and strain, discarding solids. Reserve in the fridge until ready to use. It will gel as it cools but just stir prior to using.

For each margarita, put crushed ice, 1½ ounces tequila, ½ ounce Grand Marnier, and 2 ounces cranberry puree in a shaker. Shake well. Pour drink into a sugar-rimmed martini glass. Add a cranberry swizzle stick for garnish.

ASSEMBLE CRANBERRY SWIZZLE STICKS:

In a colander rinse the cranberries. Allow to air dry. Skewer several cranberries onto each skewer but leave enough of the skewer exposed on one end to hold.

In a large cup mix light corn syrup and water to thin out syrup. Lightly brush and coat skewered cranberries with the corn syrup mixture. Sprinkle sugar over each cranberry skewer.

Place the cranberry swizzle sticks on wax paper and put in the freezer to set. These can be made about 1 hour before serving or the day before.

MAKES 10 DRINKS

VIRGIN CRANBERRY MARGARITA
Replace the tequila and Grand Marnier
with 2 ounces of sparkling cider.

PRICKLY PEAR FROZEN MARGARITA

 Grandma had several *nopales* (cactus paddles) growing along the fence in her backyard in El Paso. Together we would pick the *tunas* (prickly pears) off the cactus, peel, and eat the sweet fruit. As a tribute to my Grandma—who loved her *tunas* and *color de rosa* (the color pink)—I dedicate this beautiful pink margarita in her honor.

4 prickly pears, peeled and sliced

¼ cup water

3½ cups crushed ice

3 ounces freshly squeezed lime juice

3 ounces frozen limeade

6 ounces Silver Tequila

4½ ounces Triple Sec

3 tablespoons simple syrup (page 105)

Star fruit slices or lime wedges and coarse salt for garnish

In a blender, blend prickly pears with water to make a puree. Strain into a bowl and discard seeds.

Place crushed ice in a blender. Add prickly pear puree, lime juice, limeade, tequila, triple sec, and simple syrup; cover and pulse ingredients.

Garnish the edges of 6 margarita glasses with coarse salt. Pour pear mixture into the glasses; add a star fruit slice or a lime wedge to each glass for a garnish and serve immediately.

MAKES 6 MARGARITAS

PERSIMMON MARGARITA

 A few years ago, my husband and I were visiting his Aunt Celia in Davis, California, and she had a pile of fall fruit on her table. I noticed a bright and glossy looking fruit and picked it up. When she saw me looking at it quizzically she told me it was a persimmon. I'd never had one, and the food adventurer in me was excited to try it. I bit into it like an apple and it was love at first bite. Fast forward about fifteen years: I was standing in the produce aisle at the grocery store when I noticed gorgeous persimmons. Somehow my mind immediately shifted to cocktail hour, and I wondered if tequila and persimmons would play well together. I came to find out they do indeed dance lovingly in a margarita glass! Fall, Halloween, or *Dia de los Muertos* are the perfect times for serving these unique and vibrant orange persimmon margaritas.

1½ cups granulated sugar, divided

1 cup water

¼ cup ground cinnamon

Limes, cut into wedges and wheels

3 or 4 persimmons (See note)

2 cups tequila reposado

8 ounces lime juice

Ice cubes

In a saucepan over medium heat combine 1 cup of sugar and water. Allow the sugar to melt, making a simple syrup. Remove from heat and allow to cool. Reserve.

On a salad plate, combine the ½ cup sugar and cinnamon. Wet the rim of eight margarita or martini glasses with a lime wedge. Dip the rims of the glasses into the cinnamon mixture and coat rims evenly.

Peel the persimmons, place in a blender or juicer and puree. (You need 2 cups of puree to make 8 margaritas.)

For each drink, in a cocktail shaker, combine 2 ounces of persimmon puree, 2 ounces of tequila, 1 ounce of fresh lime juice, 2 tablespoons of simple syrup, and some ice. Give it a good shake, strain into the cinnamon-and-sugar-rimmed glass. Garnish with a lime wheel.

MAKES 8 MARGARITAS

Note: There are several persimmon varieties but the two most commonly sold in the United States are the Hachiya and Fuyu. Hachiya persimmons have an acorn shape and are usually tart until soft and ready to eat. Fuyu persimmons look like a squashed tomato, are smaller and sweeter and are edible while still firm. For the sake of this recipe we prefer the Fuyu variety.

MOJITO

Something about the mojito especially appeals to my taste buds, and this recipe will have you drinking them one right after another. From the moment I tried my first mojito, I was hooked. I even started growing my own mint just for the drink! Although this is a Cuban drink, I love that it has a universally Latin flair with lots of lime juice, mint, and, of course, rum. Stir this drink with a decorative swizzle stick or try using fresh sugarcane sticks. The muddling is the most important step in making a good mojito, so don't go bruising the mint leaves too much. All you need to do while muddling is gently press the oils from the leaves to give your mojito a potent flavor of mint. Once you've mastered the muddling, the rest falls into place easily.

12 mint leaves

2 ounces fresh lime juice

1 teaspoon powdered sugar

½ teaspoon granulated sugar

½ cup crushed ice

2 ounces white rum

2 to 3 ounces club soda, chilled

2 wedges lime, garnish

Mint sprig, garnish

Place the mint leaves in a highball glass and add the lime juice and sugars and gently muddle: press down on the mint leaves, lime juice, and sugars with a wooden spoon or muddler. Muddling releases the oils from the mint leaves. You don't want shredded leaves floating around in the drink and getting stuck between your teeth—so muddle gently.

After muddling add crushed ice and rum, and top off with club soda. Garnish with a lime wedge and a mint sprig.

MAKES 1 MOJITO

PERSIMMON MOJITO

My sister loves tequila and I love rum, so we're always thrilled about sharing our cocktail concoctions with each other. After trying the persimmon margarita recipe, Jeanine, our photographer, came up with the idea of a persimmon mojito, which I agreed was brilliant. Lots of mint and fresh lime juice makes this mojito exotically fragrant and appealing. Persimmons are in season from September through December and are at their peak in November, making this a perfect drink during the fall and winter. One sip of this light, refreshing mojito and your mind willingly escapes to the Caribbean.

1 persimmon (recommend Fuyu variety)

10 mint leaves

4 tablespoons fresh lime juice

½ cup crushed ice

3 tablespoons simple syrup (page 105)

2 ounces light rum

Club soda

Lime slices

Mint sprig for garnish (optional)

Peel the persimmon, place in a blender or juicer and puree. Reserve. Put the mint and lime juice in a muddler. Muddle just long enough to release the mint oils.

Place the crushed ice in a high ball glass. Add 3 tablespoons persimmon puree, muddled lime juice and mint leaves, simple syrup, and rum. Top with club soda. Stir gently and serve garnished with a lime slice and mint sprig.

VARIATION: VIRGIN PERSIMMON MOJITO

This is a great virgin drink for adults, but let's be honest, it's perfect for our kiddos too!

1 persimmon (recommend Fuyu variety), peeled and pureed

10 mint leaves, muddled

4 tablespoons fresh lime juice

4 ounces lemon-lime soda

Crushed ice

Lime slices

Place some crushed ice in a high ball glass. Add 3 tablespoons persimmon puree and the muddled mint and lime juice, and top off with lemon-lime soda and stir gently.

Serve garnished with a lime slice and mint sprig.

MAKES 1 MOJITO

WARM PEAR CIDER
CALIENTITO

 I love natural serveware and had a fun idea about how to serve this *calientito* (warm drink): in a hollowed-out Asian pear! It's much more charming and "green" than a plastic tumbler, and you can even nibble the pear when you're done. The fusion of tequila with the trilogy of winter spices—cinnamon, cloves, and anise—is a warm and cozy combination that soothes both the throat and stomach. As you prepare this drink, your entire home will smell delicious, beckoning visitors. What a great way to welcome your holiday guests—with a delicately prepared Asian pear filled with the warmth of winter.

3½ cups pear nectar

1 or 2 cinnamon sticks

3 whole cloves

4 whole anise stars

¾ cup tequila gold or reposado

4 to 6 Asian pears (optional)

Combine pear nectar, cinnamon sticks, cloves, and anise stars in a medium saucepan. Bring to a boil, then reduce heat and simmer for 10 to 15 minutes.

Add tequila and stir to incorporate.

Cut off the pear tops and with a sharp knife carefully outline a rim on your pear cups. With a melon baller or a spoon, hollow out the pears making sure to leave about ¼ inch at the bottom and around the edges, creating a cup.

Pour warm nectar into pear cups and enjoy!

MAKES 4 TO 6 DRINKS

LA LLORONA

 This intoxicating drink was inspired by a Halloween night when I was using dry ice in a punch bowl. The eerie trail of wispy smoke created by the dry ice looked like the long, flowing gown worn by *La Llorona*. *La Llorona*, according to ancient Mexican folklore, was a beautiful woman who drowned her children to be with a man and when he wanted nothing to do with her, she lost her mind. In the afterlife, she walks up and down bodies of water, wailing and looking for her children. It's a conversation starter for a Halloween party, but you can skip the dry ice for a yummy drink year-round.

3 ounces Pisco Brandy

1 ounce fresh lime juice

1 ounce fresh lemon juice

1½ tablespoons granulated sugar

Dash of Angostoria bitters

Crushed ice

Dry ice (optional) (see note)

In a cocktail shaker filled with crushed ice, combine brandy, juices, and sugar. Cover, shake vigorously for 15 seconds, and strain into a cocktail glass. Top with a few drops of bitters. Add some dry ice for a spooky effect.

MAKES 1 DRINK

Note: Dry ice is quite safe to use in drinks, but you should not touch it. Wait for the ice to melt before actually drinking it as it can burn your skin.

EL CHUPACABRA MARTINI

 Translated into English as "the Goat Sucker," *El Chupacabra* is a mythical creature known for its nocturnal prowling and as the culprit in weird livestock deaths. There are various descriptions of the creature, which is believed to be heavy and the size of a small bear with a row of spines stretching from head to tail. Maybe you've heard the silly stories. My fascination with this mythical creature inspired me to invent a drink as its namesake. This martini is infused with fiery red blood orange juice and the explosive Brazilian aphrodisiac açaí, making this an exotic bright red cocktail full of drama and flavor. Açaí juice is actually very healthy and has 33 times the antioxidant content of red wine grapes. Hints of guava and pineapple nectar in this drink are fruits from Puerto Rico (where *Chupacabra* sightings were first reported). The understated tones of coconut rum make this drink equally dangerous, so sip with caution.

Freshly squeezed juice of 4 blood oranges or
  1 cup orange juice

4 ounces coconut rum

2 ounces açaí juice

1 ounce guava nectar

1 ounce pineapple nectar

1 cup crushed ice

1 blood orange, sliced, for garnish

1 star fruit, sliced (optional), for garnish

In a cocktail shaker combine all ingredients with ice. Shake until blended and then strain into 2 martini glasses.

Garnish each glass with a blood orange slice or a star fruit slice. Serve.

MAKES 2 DRINKS

SANDIATINI

Sandia (watermelon) lends itself to so many refreshing, easy recipes during the hot months of summer and this is one of them. All you have to do is prepare *Agua de Sandia* (Watermelon Cooler) and you have the base for this grown-up cocktail. It's the drink that keeps on giving. Serve the *Agua de Sandia* to the kids during the day, then add a splash of coconut rum and club soda and serve it to adults at night. *Salud!*

3 ounces coconut rum

3 ounces Agua de Sandia (page 101)

1 ounce club soda, pre-chilled

Ice

Mint leaves

Pour the rum, agua de sandia, and club soda into a cocktail shaker. Toss in a handful of ice cubes and shake vigorously. Strain into a chilled martini glass and garnish with mint.

MAKES 1 DRINK

MEXICAN FRUIT SANGRIA
SANGRIA MEXICANA

 The single most important ingredient in sangria has to be the wine, but don't forget what a key role the fruit plays. The colorful palette of oranges, lemons, limes, apples, and pears bathing in a sea of Spanish red wine beckons like no other drink. I love to eat the succulent fruit after the sangria is all gone. Each slice is laden with all the sweet and smoky notes from both the brandy and the wine. A glass of sangria goes well with just about any dish. However, the playful combination of fruit from trees and fruit of the vine pairs perfectly with most spicy dishes.

2 bottles of red wine (recommend Rioja)

2 cups brandy

1 cup fresh orange juice

1 orange, sliced

1 lemon, sliced

1 lime, sliced

1 apple, cored and cut into thin wedges

1 pear, cored and cut into thin wedges

1 (750-ml) bottle club soda, chilled

Ice

Combine the wine, brandy, orange juice, and fruits in a large container or glass pitcher. Cover and chill completely, at least 1 to 2 hours or overnight.

Add soda to mixture when ready to serve. Serve with ice and some of the fruit.

15 SERVINGS

CHELADA

When I tasted my first *chelada* I thought, "Where has this drink been all of my life?" Limes, limes, and more limes make this drink oh-so-refreshing. I have seen and tested several variations and the combination of limes, beer, and other ingredients can set off an entire group of *chelada* and *michelada* drinkers debating over the exact ingredients and origin for this drink. Sometimes I like mine with spicy tomato juice, which is more of a traditional *michelada*, but most of the time I like it simple, with only freshly squeezed lime juice and a salt rim.

Coarse salt

¼ cup ice

¼ cup fresh lime juice

1 bottle (12 ounces) Mexican beer (recommend Dos XX or Tecate)

Moisten rim of glass with a lime and coat with salt. Add ice and lime juice. Pour in beer and drink before the ice melts.

MAKES 1 DRINK

KAHLÚA CAFÉ

I always think of this café as a dessert. I guess anything topped with a dollop of whipped cream deserves that distinction. Add a shot of Kahlúa and you have the perfectly brewed after-dinner drink. Any way you whip it up, it's a darn good *cafecito* before or after a meal. If you like the flavor of cinnamon as much as I do, try using a cinnamon stick to mix in the cream. The hint of cinnamon is subtle and does not overpower the flavor of the coffee. Not only is this coffee a feast for the eyes, but it is a satisfyingly sweet treat for the taste buds!

1 10-to-12-cup pot of freshly brewed coffee

½ pint heavy whipping cream

1 bottle of Kahlúa

1 dark or milk chocolate bar, grated or shaved

10 to 12 cinnamon sticks

Brew your coffee to your liking. I prefer French-pressed coffee.

Pour the whipping cream into a bowl and whip with a hand blender until light and fluffy.

For each serving, pour some coffee into a favorite coffee mug; add 1 ounce of Kahlúa, and top off with a dollop of whipped cream. Sprinkle some of the grated chocolate on the whipped cream, add a cinnamon stick, and enjoy this warm cup of coffee with dessert.

MAKES 10 TO 12 CUPS

CHOCOLATE ATOLE
CHAMPURRADO

Warm, chocolaty *champurrado* is synonymous with tamales and cold mornings, especially on *Las Posadas*, *Dia de los Muertos*, and *Navidad*. These are the most common times family recipes came out of the recipe box—or Grandma's kitchen. I fondly remember drinking it on cold mornings in my Grandma's house. It was usually too hot to drink so she would cool it off by pouring it from one cup to another over the sink. *Champurrado* is a chocolate drink with a bold taste of corn. The consistency is like that of a thin cream of wheat. This is a heavy drink and sometimes it was all we had for breakfast and sometimes it was all we needed.

3 cups of water

2 cinnamon sticks

1 anise star

¼ cup masa harina (corn flour)

2 cups milk

1.5 ounces Mexican chocolate (recommend Nestle-Abuelita), chopped

3 ounces piloncillo, chopped (or substitute ½ cup packed brown sugar)

In a large saucepan bring water to a boil with the cinnamon sticks and anise star. Remove from the heat, cover, and let the cinnamon sticks and anise star steep for about 1 hour.

Remove the cinnamon sticks and anise star, return water to low heat, and slowly add the masa harina, whisking until combined. Add milk, chocolate, and piloncillo.

Heat over medium heat just until boiling. Reduce heat and simmer, uncovered, whisking occasionally, about 10 minutes, or until chocolate is completely melted and sugar is dissolved. Serve immediately.

6 SERVINGS

CINNAMON HOT CHOCOLATE
CHOCOLATE CALIENTE CON CANELA

 We used to have this hot drink on cold mornings with our breakfast or on winter evenings. *Mi mamá* used to make it for us, especially when all my nieces and nephews would spend the night. The full pot of hot chocolate would go a long way and it was very inexpensive for her to make. The scent of cinnamon boiling gave us the first hint that she was making this wonderful chocolate treat for us. When my kids were little I used to make it every winter, especially around Thanksgiving and Christmas. When they come home to visit for the holidays I always make a double batch and still it's never enough. This drink warms you up from the inside out and drinking it together with my children over the holidays is the perfect excuse to reminisce about the good ol' days.

8½ cups water, divided

3 cinnamon sticks

5 tablespoons cocoa powder

4 tablespoons cornstarch

1 cup evaporated low-fat or whole milk

8 tablespoons granulated sugar

Bring 8¼ cups of water with cinnamon sticks to a boil; remove from heat, cover, and let steep for 1 hour.

Discard cinnamon sticks and return water to medium-low heat. Add cocoa powder and stir until dissolved.

In a separate cup, dissolve cornstarch in ¼ cup of cold water. Stir to prevent clumps and add to pot, stirring as you pour it in.

Add the milk and sugar and let it come to a slow boil, being careful to turn off heat as soon as it boils. It will thicken a little and will be creamier with whole milk.

7 TO 8 SERVINGS

aguas y
paletas

RICE AND CINNAMON DRINK
AGUA DE HORCHATA

 *Horchata* is a drink made primarily with rice and spices. Although it is white in color and creamy, it usually does not contain milk. My children and grandchildren love this very old, traditional drink. If I don't have time to make it when they come to visit I know we can always buy some at a Mexican restaurant or a Latin grocery store. In Spain *horchata* is made with *chufa* (tiger nut) but in Mexico it's made with rice. Most Latin families that make it have their own special twists.

My niece Georgina shared her recipe with me, and I gave it a few tweaks (using simple syrup instead of granulated sugar and pulverizing the rice beforehand to eliminate chalky sediment and a gritty taste). Grinding the rice also helps thicken the drink.

1 cup uncooked long-grain white rice

6 cups water

1 cinnamon stick

2 whole cloves

½ teaspoon pure vanilla extract

2 cups medium simple syrup (page 105)

In a food processor or coffee grinder, pulverize the rice so it is the consistency of ground coffee.

In a large saucepan over high heat, bring the water to a boil. Remove from heat; add ground rice, cinnamon stick, and cloves. Cover and let soak for 8 hours or overnight at room temperature.

After soaking, break the cinnamon stick in half, and place the rice mixture in a blender. Puree for 2 to 3 minutes.

Strain the liquid by pouring it into a fine strainer lined with a double layer of cheesecloth set over a pitcher. Squeeze out any excess liquid into the pitcher and discard the solids.

Stir in the vanilla and medium simple syrup. Cover and refrigerate until you're ready to serve. Stir before pouring into glasses and serve over ice.

MAKES 4 TO 5 CUPS

WATERMELON COOLER
AGUA DE SANDIA

Because watermelons are so inexpensive during the summer months and both grocery stores and farmers markets are flooded with them, why not try making a cold pitcher of what we call *agua de sandia*, which literally translated means "watermelon water." It's almost like having a smoothie without the milk. After you make some for the kids, be sure to try our adult version, Sandiatini (page 85).

8 cups cubed and seeded watermelon

¼ cup water

¼ cup fresh lime juice

1¾ cups light simple syrup (page 105)

2 limes, sliced for garnish

Mint leaves for garnish

Puree half of the cubed watermelon and water in a blender. Pour through a course strainer and into a large pitcher. Repeat with the remaining watermelon and water.

Stir in lime juice. Add simple syrup. Stir and add more simple syrup according to how sweet you want it.

Refrigerate until very cold. Stir before serving and garnish with lime slices and mint if desired.

MAKES 2 QUARTS

HIBISCUS TEA
AGUA DE JAMAICA

This ruby red tea is easily made from dry hibiscus flowers purchased in packages or in bulk at a Latin grocery store. *Agua de jamaica* (pronounced ha-mike-ah) is a surprisingly thirst-quenching drink. Like iced tea, you can make it as sweet or as light as you desire. Try making ice cubes from the tea itself so when added to the glass the tea doesn't get watered down. Another way to use *agua de jamaica* is to add some simple syrup to sweeten it up a little more and make popsicles. (See page 104 for a popsicle recipe.)

8 cups water

¼ cup dried hibiscus flowers (jamaica)

½ cup granulated sugar (more if desired)

Ice

Mint leaves (optional)

Rinse and drain the dried hibiscus flowers in a large colander.

Bring water to a boil in a pot. Add the flowers and cover tightly with a lid. Remove from the heat and steep for 1 hour or until cool.

Strain hibiscus water into a pitcher and discard flowers. Add sugar and stir. Refrigerate until time to serve. Ladle into a tall glass filled with ice and garnish with fresh mint leaves (optional).

MAKES 2 QUARTS

POPSICLES
PALETAS

We love *paletas* (popsicles) probably as much as our kids do. These simple recipes demystify the popsicle-making process. If you make some of our *aguas* (Mexican coolers) then you can easily make popsicles. And if you plan ahead during hot summer months, you can always have some *paletas* ready for that scorching day when all you want is something cold and refreshing. I also love an ice cold *paleta* after a spicy dinner. Adding chunks of fruit to any of the following *paleta* recipes makes it that much better. Below are some of my favorite recipes for *limón* (lime), *coco* (coconut), *sandia* (watermelon), *jamaica* (hibiscus), and *horchata* (rice and cinnamon drink) *paletas*.

LEMON-LIME POPSICLES / PALETAS DE LIMÓN

Juice of 6 lemons
Juice of 6 limes
1½ cups simple syrup
Peel of 3 lemons, grated
Peel of 3 limes, grated

WATERMELON POPSICLES / PALETAS DE SANDIA

1¼ cups Agua de Sandia (page 101)
1 cup simple syrup

COCONUT POPSICLES / PALETAS DE COCO

3 cups coconut milk
1½ cups simple syrup
3 teaspoons coconut extract

HIBISCUS POPSICLES / PALETAS DE JAMAICA

1¼ cups Agua de Jamaica (page 103)
1 cup simple syrup

In a mixing bowl combine all the ingredients for your chosen flavor. Fill six popsicle molds (see note page 107). Place in the freezer for at least 4 hours or overnight.

MAKES 6 POPSICLES, 3 OUNCES EACH

SIMPLE SYRUP

Simple syrup (medium) is made with equal parts sugar and water. Light simple syrup is made the same way but with 2 parts water and 1 part sugar.

2 cups granulated sugar

2 cups water

Combine sugar and water in a saucepan over low heat. Cook just long enough for the sugar to melt. Remove from heat and let cool. Store any unused simple syrup in the refrigerator. Makes about 2½ cups.

Horchata

HORCHATA POPSICLES
PALETAS DE HORCHATA

 To avoid any rice settling in our *paletas*, which occurs with *horchata*, for this recipe we prefer to use commercial rice milk and some added cinnamon. You can always use our *horchata* recipe (page 99), just take note that some settling of rice particles will occur at the bottom of the popsicle mold. Either way, *horchata* popsicles are worth the effort.

1 cup water

1 cup granulated sugar

2 cinnamon sticks

1 ¼ cup vanilla rice milk (recommend Rice Dream)

Bring water to a boil over high heat, add sugar and mix while it melts, about 1 minute. Remove from heat, add cinnamon sticks, cover, and let steep for about 2 hours. (Will make about 1 ¼ cups.)

In a mixing bowl combine 1 cup cinnamon-infused simple syrup and rice milk. Fill six popsicle molds. Place in the freezer for about 4 hours or overnight.

MAKES 6 POPSICLES

Note: There are lots of companies out there that sell popsicle molds. For these recipes we use the traditional paleta mold. You can also use little disposable plastic or paper cups with wooden popsicle sticks. Remember the little Dixie cups? Those work great. If you are using a traditional plastic popsicle mold with a cover to keep the wooden popsicle sticks in place you should soak the wooden sticks in water for about 30 minutes first. Doing this will keep the popsicle sticks from floating to the surface during the freezing process. If you are not using a popsicle mold you will need to freeze the popsicles without the sticks for about 30 minutes. After 30 minutes add the popsicle sticks. This will keep the sticks upright in the popsicle as they finish freezing.

appetizers

BRUSCHETTA TOPPED WITH APRICOT, MELTED BRIE, AND POMEGRANATE SEEDS

Grandma had two *granada* (pomegranate) trees in her backyard and as a kid I would stare at those trees for any sign of ripened fruit. Once I'd spot one I would pester Grandma until she allowed me to pick it. As I would cut the fruit open the slippery seeds popped and splashed on the wall and floor. Grandma was never upset about the mess I left behind. She would encourage me to get all the seeds out and put them in a cup so we could eat them together. As an adult I have learned a mess-free way to open those lovely, fresh pomegranates. I wish I had known this clever trick when I was a kid.

Now *granadas* always remind me of my Grandma. I love cheese, and I especially love it with fruit. The combination of brie with apricot preserves and pomegranate seeds is divine! Goat brie, with its creamy, tangy, and slightly salty flavor, works especially well in this recipe, and the pomegranate seeds add enough tartness and crunch to balance out the mildness of the cheese. The best thing about this recipe is that it's easy enough to prepare just before your guests arrive. Cheese lovers are sure to fall in love at first bite.

1 large pomegranate

2 cloves garlic, sliced

2 tablespoons olive oil

1 French baguette

1 cup apricot preserves

4 ounces soft-ripened Brie cheese (recommend goat Brie)

Rosemary sprigs for garnish

Break open the pomegranate in a bowl of water to free the seeds. The seeds will sink to the bottom of the bowl and the rest will float to the top. Discard the white membrane and put the seeds in a separate bowl. Reserve 1 cup of the seeds and set aside.

Preheat oven to 400 degrees F.

Place garlic slices in olive oil and microwave for 1 minute to infuse the olive oil with garlic. Cut the baguette into ½-inch-thick slices. Brush infused olive oil on one side of baguette slices. Lay slices on a baking sheet and place in the preheated oven. Bake for 5 to 6 minutes. (The bread does not need to brown, just creating toast-like crust on the top surface is enough.)

Spread apricot preserves on toasted bread. Microwave Brie cheese for 10 to 15 seconds to soften. Cut the Brie in half and spoon or drizzle the cheese on the toasted bread. Place 1 teaspoon of pomegranate seeds on each slice. Serve while warm and garnish plate with rosemary sprigs.

MAKES 24 PIECES

BACON-WRAPPED SHRIMP WITH JALAPEÑO

CAMARONES BROCHETTE

Everything tastes better with bacon, and these decadent small bites are no exception. Who wouldn't love the salty, smoky crunch of bacon with shrimp? These appetizers complement any dinner party or barbecue—whether you're planning on cooking indoors or outdoors on the grill. These perfect little bites will be devoured as quickly as you can make them, so plan accordingly and double your recipe. Try adding a side of *salsa verde* (page 59) for dunking!

1 pound bacon

½ cup salted butter, melted

3 teaspoons tequila

1 teaspoon lime juice

1 teaspoon garlic powder

½ teaspoon ground black pepper

½ teaspoon dried Mexican oregano

20 medium-large shrimp (about 1 pound)

3 jalapeño peppers, cut into thin strips

Wooden toothpicks, presoaked

Preheat broiler. Microwave bacon on high for 1 minute. Separate slices and cut slices in half crosswise and let cool.

In a bowl, combine melted butter, tequila, lime juice, garlic powder, pepper, and oregano.

Peel the shrimp, butterfly, and devein, leaving the tail and last section intact. Place 2 jalapeño strips in each shrimp and press sides together. Wrap a half slice of bacon around each shrimp and secure with a toothpick. Use a pastry brush to coat the shrimp with butter mixture.

Place bacon-wrapped shrimp evenly on a foil-lined cookie sheet. Place under broiler. Broil for 6 minutes, turning over after 3 minutes. The crispiness of the bacon and shrimp edges is scrumptious.

VARIATION: This is a great recipe to make on the grill. Instead of using a toothpick you can skewer 3 to 4 shrimp per skewer. (If using wooden skewers, don't forget to soak skewers about 30 minutes before using.) Place crosswise on the grates and grill for about 3 to 4 minutes on each side. Remove from skewers and serve warm.

MAKES ABOUT 20

CORN IN A CUP
ELOTE EN VASO

This is Mexico's finest street dish, often sold in styrofoam cups. Growing up in the border city of El Paso, I saw *elote en vaso* sold at street corners, bazaars, and festivals. When I moved away from home I craved these steaming corn kernels drenched in melted butter and aromatic lime juice, topped with crumbly cheese. This is a very simple recipe that produces a comforting Mexican classic. Feel free to adjust the proportions of lime juice, *crema*, cheese, and spices to taste.

10 ears corn

3 sticks (24 tablespoons) salted butter

3 cups lime juice

3 cups crema Mexicana or sour cream

Chili powder to taste

Salt to taste

Hot sauce (optional; recommend Valentina
    Mexican Hot Sauce)

12 ounces crumbly, salty white cheese (ideally
    cotija but parmesan is acceptable)

Lime wedges for garnish

Husk the corn, remove the silks, and slice the kernels from the cobs with a sharp knife. Place the corn in a saucepan with enough salted water to cover. Bring to a boil; let boil for 2 to 3 minutes, then drain. Turn off the heat and return corn to saucepan.

For each serving: Put ¾ cup of corn in a glass. Add 2 tablespoons of butter and stir to melt the butter. Mix in ¼ cup lime juice and ¼ cup crema. Sprinkle with a good heavy coating of chili powder and salt if desired, though the cheese adds plenty of salt. If you like spicy then add a few drops of some hot sauce for that extra kick of heat. Mix well. Top with 2 tablespoons crumbled cheese.

Serve with a spoon and lime wedges.

12 SERVINGS

GUACAMOLE

We love avocados and although there are many ways of preparing them our favorite is a pure and simple guacamole. Stay away from powders or imitation anything on this recipe and the end result will be a delicious combination of seven simple ingredients. Chunks of avocado, onions, and tomatoes make a beautiful, delicious presentation, so be careful not to over mash.

4 ripe avocados

1 clove garlic, minced

¼ cup minced white onion

1 jalapeño pepper, minced (optional)

1 tablespoon salt

1 medium tomato, chopped

1 to 2 tablespoons fresh lime juice

Cut the avocado in half. Twist to pull apart and remove the pit. Scoop out the flesh. Place in a medium bowl and mash the avocado with a fork leaving some chunks.

Add the garlic, onion, jalapeño (optional), salt, and tomato. Squeeze the lime juice over all the ingredients and give everything a gentle stir, but don't overdo it.

VARIATION: If you own a molcajete (lava-stone mortar), using the tejolote (lava-stone pestle) grind the garlic, onion, jalapeño, and salt until all the ingredients are well ground. Dice the avocados and gently fold into the garlic-onion-chile paste, keeping the avocados fairly intact. Add tomatoes and squeeze the lime juice over the avocado and gently stir until the mixture is chunky. Taste and add salt, if necessary. Serve immediately, directly from the molcajete (or bowl), with tortilla chips.

8 SERVINGS

MEXICAN CHORIZO AND CHEESE
QUESO FUNDIDO CON CHORIZO

Who can resist warm, melted cheese? Add spicy chorizo and a splash of tequila and you have our *queso fundido favorito*. Adding a flame to the tequila allows the alcohol to burn off, leaving a smoky, richly flavored cheese spread. Sometimes when I go out with friends, all we order are cheese dishes like this one, a mountain of warm corn tortillas, and a few *cervezas*. It really is all you need for a wonderful evening. Oh, and don't forget the Mexican music in the background. Here's our version for creating this at home.

5 ounces Mexican chorizo, casings removed

½ cup sliced white onion (½-inch strips)

½ cup silver/blanco tequila

12 ounces quesadilla or asadero cheese, shredded

1 tablespoon chopped cilantro

6 corn or flour tortillas, warmed

Preheat oven to 350 degrees F.

In an oven-safe iron skillet, cook the chorizo on your stovetop until almost done, about 15 minutes. Drain excess fat.

Add the onion to the chorizo and cook until browned. Remove pan from the heat.

Carefully add tequila. Return to heat and simmer, uncovered, for 15 to 20 seconds or until most of the tequila has dissipated. Remove from heat.

Stir in the cheese and combine well. Place skillet in the oven and bake uncovered for about 10 to 15 minutes or until cheese is completely melted and slightly golden brown on top.

Sprinkle with fresh cilantro. Serve with corn or flour tortillas.

6 SERVINGS

Note: If you need to double the recipe, do not double the tequila, use only ½ cup.

ROASTED GREEN CHILES WITH BUTTERMILK AND CHEESE
RAJAS CON SUERO Y QUESO ASADERO

 *Mi mamá* always made this delicious staple to eat with *frijoles de la olla* (page 215). The *suero* (whey) has made this recipe uniquely ours and gives the green chile a creamy tang and perfect saltiness. We especially love this dish as a part of our Thanksgiving menu. In fact, she made this dish for us for our last Thanksgiving celebration with her, two months before she passed away. I roasted the green chiles and she peeled off the skins. She sat in her wheelchair at the kitchen table, where she always loved to be, giving me instructions. I hope your family enjoys this unique chile dish as much as we do!

1 tablespoon olive oil

½ Spanish yellow onion, chopped

3 cloves garlic, chopped, or 1 tablespoon garlic powder

1 tomato, chopped (optional)

1 tablespoon flour

13 Anaheim chiles, roasted and peeled (see page 20), thinly sliced

1 to 2 jalapeño peppers, roasted and peeled (see page 20), chopped (optional for extra spice)

2½ cups suero (whey) or buttermilk

2 cups shredded asadero cheese

Salt to taste

Heat oil in a large skillet, add onions and cook, stirring, until translucent, about 2 minutes.

Add garlic and cook for 1 minute, stirring constantly so as not to burn the garlic.

Add tomato (optional) and stir. Add flour and stir for another 2 minutes.

Add the roasted Anaheim chiles and jalapeño peppers and let simmer for 2 minutes, stirring constantly to combine all the flavors together.

Add the suero and bring to a boil. Stir in the cheese. Cover and remove from the heat. Allow the cheese to melt before serving. Add salt to taste.

12 TO 14 SERVINGS

SHRIMP CEVICHE
CEVICHE DE CAMERON

Ceviche is seafood marinated in citric juices such as lemons and limes. We did not grow up near the beach and hardly ate any fish. But after leaving El Paso I began to eat more seafood and quickly fell in love with it, especially shrimp. The first time I ate ceviche was in my early twenties in Mazatlan and I decided to recreate the magic back home. This ceviche is very simple and fresh. The best part is that there is no cooking involved and so it is perfect to make in the heat of summer. It's a great appetizer with tortilla chips, or as a light meal served on *tostadas*.

4 pounds large raw tiger shrimp

Juice of 6 limes

Juice of 4 lemons

4 vine-ripened tomatoes, seeded and chopped

1 small red onion, chopped

2 serrano peppers, finely chopped

1 cucumber, peeled, seeded, and chopped

Handful cilantro, chopped, plus several sprigs for garnish

2 avocados, peeled, pitted, and cubed

1 teaspoon olive oil

1 teaspoon salt

¼ teaspoon ground black pepper

2 bags tortilla chips or whole tostadas

Peel, devein, and cut shrimp into ¼-inch pieces.

Spread out the shrimp in a glass baking dish. Pour lime and lemon juice over shrimp, toss well, and refrigerate for 2 hours, mixing occasionally. The acid from the limes and lemons will "cook" the shrimp.

Toss prepared shrimp with juices with the remaining ingredients (except tortilla chips) and refrigerate for 1 hour or longer. You can even prepare this the night before, allowing all the flavors to fuse together overnight.

Serve cold with tortilla chips or whole tostadas.

MAKES 10½ CUPS

MEXICAN SHRIMP COCKTAIL
CÓCTEL DE CAMARONES

 My mother used to make this spicy shrimp cocktail for Christmas Eve or New Years Eve parties. She also used to sell her Mexican shrimp cocktail at our family grocery store. She would make it daily and sold it in clear plastic cups with a side of saltine crackers. A bottle of Tabasco sat on the counter for customers to spice up their own cup. It was a *barrio* (neighborhood) favorite. The spicy cocktail sauce made with freshly chopped red onions, cilantro, and avocados is the perfect light and easy appetizer or healthy lunch, especially during hot months.

½ cup ketchup

1½ cups vegetable juice (recommend V8)

1 to 2 tablespoons horseradish (add more or less according to spicy tolerance)

Juice of 2 limes

½ teaspoon bottled hot sauce (recommend Tabasco)

⅛ teaspoon garlic powder

¼ cup finely chopped red onion

¼ cup chopped cilantro

1 pound small shrimp, shelled, deveined, and cooked

1 avocado, pitted, peeled, and finely chopped

Saltine crackers or tortilla chips, for serving

Stir together the ketchup, vegetable juice, horseradish, lime juice, hot sauce, and garlic powder until well blended. Taste and add more horseradish or hot sauce if you would like it spicier.

Add the onion, cilantro, and shrimp and mix well. Gently stir in the avocado.

Cover and refrigerate 2 to 3 hours.

Serve in 4-ounce glasses with saltine crackers or tortilla chips.

4 TO 6 SERVINGS

soups

MEXICAN MEATBALL SOUP
ALBONDIGAS

Albondigas is a very traditional Mexican meatball soup. Yup, Mexican meatballs, who knew? The exotic trio of cilantro, coriander, and safflower petals gives this soup its distinctive flavor. I say if it doesn't have these three spices it's not *albondiga* soup. Some soups are great before the main course, but this soup is the meal. With the carefully crafted meatballs, bountiful vegetables, and rice you will be more than satisfied. I fondly remember my grandmother rolling out each little meatball. I always wondered how she managed to make every miniature meatball the exact same size. Next time you want the perfect cold weather meal, try a hefty serving of *albondiga* soup, a tall pile of freshly made corn tortillas, and a little *salsa casera*. *Aye que bueno*.

MEATBALLS

1 pound lean ground beef

1 teaspoon garlic powder

1 teaspoon salt

1 teaspoon ground black pepper

¼ cup chopped yellow onion

¼ cup long-grain rice

SOUP

2 (32-ounce) cartons chicken broth
   (recommend low sodium)

2 cups water

Salt to taste

1 tablespoon olive oil

¼ cup long grain rice

½ cup chopped yellow onion

2 large tomatoes, chopped

4 cloves garlic, chopped

2 to 3 potatoes, cubed

2 large carrots, peeled and sliced

3 celery stalks, chopped

¼ cup tomato sauce

¼ teaspoon crushed coriander seeds

3 to 4 tablespoons chopped cilantro

½ teaspoon safflower petals (azafran)

Cilantro sprigs and lime wedges for garnish

(CONTINUED)

MEXICAN MEATBALL SOUP

(CONTINUED)

PREPARE MEATBALLS:

In a large mixing bowl combine ground beef with garlic powder, salt, black pepper, onions, and rice. Mix all ingredients together and roll out about 36 to 40 1-inch meatballs.

MAKE SOUP:

In a large pot, bring broth and water to a boil with salt. Lower heat to medium and carefully drop meatballs into water. Cook meatballs for about 10 to 15 minutes or until meatballs float to the surface, then lower heat to simmer.

In skillet, over medium heat, add oil. Add rice and cook for about 2 minutes. Add onions and sauté until translucent, about 2 minutes.

Add tomatoes and garlic to skillet and continue to cook for another 3 minutes. Add entire skillet contents to meatball pot.

Add potatoes, carrots, and celery to meatball pot. Simmer over medium heat until vegetables are cooked, about 20 minutes.

Add tomato sauce, coriander seeds, cilantro, and safflower petals and allow to come to a boil so all the flavors come together, about 10 minutes.

Ladle soup with about 5 meatballs per bowl.

Garnish with cilantro sprigs and lime wedges, and serve with warm corn tortillas (page 41). If you would like your soup spicy, add a spoonful of salsa casera (page 60).

6 TO 8 SERVINGS

HOMEMADE CHICKEN SOUP
CALDO DE POLLO

This was one of *mi mamá's* favorite dishes on cold winter days, or when we had a cold or the flu. It warms you to the core and soothes those annoying body aches that show up during cold season. She would also make this soup on wash days, so she would not have to spend too much time in the kitchen while she was busy washing clothes. Wash day for her meant a full day of washing clothes with a washboard, hanging them outside on the line to dry, folding them, and finally ironing piles of clothes. I know a bowl of this restorative soup was the perfect meal after that hard day's work!

8 cups water

4 to 6 skinless chicken drumsticks or thighs

1 tablespoon salt

4 cloves garlic, chopped

1 tablespoon olive oil

¼ cup white long-grain rice

½ cup chopped onion

2 roma tomatoes, chopped

2 carrots, sliced

3 celery stalks, sliced

3 Yukon Gold potatoes, quartered

⅓ cup tomato sauce

1 tablespoon chopped cilantro

¼ teaspoon safflower petals (azafran)

Lime wedges

In a large (at least 10-quart) pot, put the water, chicken, salt, and garlic. Boil for 15 minutes.

While the chicken is boiling, in a separate pan, heat the oil over medium heat, add rice and cook, stirring occasionally, until browned, about 2 to 3 minutes, being careful not to let it burn. Add onion and continue cooking until onion is translucent, about 2 minutes. Add tomato and cook for an additional 3 minutes. Add mixture to chicken pot.

Add carrots, celery, and potatoes to soup and let come to a boil; reduce heat. Let simmer until vegetables cook through, about 20 to 30 minutes. Add tomato sauce, cilantro, and safflower petals during the last 5 minutes. Ladle soup, including a piece of chicken for each serving, into bowls and serve with lime wedges, warm corn tortillas (page 41), and salsa casera (page 60).

4 TO 6 SERVINGS

BEEF SOUP
CALDO DE RES

This was one of my mother Jesusita's favorite dishes to prepare on Sundays when all her children would visit after church. She lived near the Catholic church that most of our family grew up attending and so everyone would drop by after mass. Along with her *frijoles de la olla* (page 215), green or red chile with beef, *arroz* (page 223), *salsa casera* (page 60), and of course, her hot-off-the-*comal* homemade flour tortillas (page 43), this beef soup always had a place on the table. Those were days I will cherish forever, all my siblings around the table with our beautiful *mamá*.

11 cups water

1½ pounds soup bones

1½ pounds beef shank bones, cut into 3 or 4 pieces

1 tablespoon salt

3 cloves garlic, chopped

½ white or yellow onion, cut in 1-inch squares

½ head of cabbage, chopped

1 large carrot, sliced

2 celery stalks, sliced

2 Yukon Gold potatoes, peeled and cubed

2 Mexican zucchini, sliced

2 tomatoes, chopped

1 fresh corn on the cob, cut into 1-inch slices

¼ cup tomato sauce

¼ teaspoon safflower petals (azafran)

¼ teaspoon whole coriander seeds, crushed

3 tablespoons chopped cilantro

3 limes, cut into wedges (optional)

Over high heat in a large stockpot, bring water to a boil.

Add soup bones, shank bones, salt, garlic, and onion and boil for about 10 minutes. Lower heat to low, cover pot, and simmer for about 2½ to 3 hours or until meat on bones is tender. Skim excess foam off the top as it forms and discard.

Add cabbage, carrots, celery, potatoes, zucchini, tomatoes, corn, tomato sauce, safflower petals, coriander seeds, and cilantro. Let it all cook for about 30 minutes, until potatoes are soft but not mushy.

Serve with Mexican rice and lime wedges on the side, and don't forget the corn tortillas.

8 TO 9 SERVINGS

CHICKEN TORTILLA SOUP
SOPA AZTECA

My adorable *gringo* husband is the one who actually came up with this recipe. He loves tortilla soup and enjoyed experimenting with the roasting of several ingredients before coming up with this final and aromatic recipe. The broth, the broth, the broth—that's what gives this soup its *sabor fabuloso*. This is one of those recipes where you must roast the tomatoes because the tortilla, along with the smokiness of the tomatoes, gives it its unique flavor. The use of fewer vegetables brings the broth front and center. The delicate and harmonious combination of the roasted tomatoes and the fried tortillas allows one to savor the flavor of the corn and the chiles.

10 cups water

2 chicken breasts

2 chicken thighs

3 tablespoons salt

3 tablespoons olive oil, divided

2 pasilla or ancho chiles, stemmed, seeded, and torn into large pieces

4 medium tomatoes

½ medium yellow onion, coarsely chopped

1 clove garlic

Ground black pepper to taste

⅓ cup canola oil, for frying tortilla strips

14 white or yellow corn tortillas, sliced into ¼-inch-thick strips

2 avocados, pitted, peeled, and diced

2 cups shredded quesadilla or asadero cheese (optional)

Shredded cabbage (optional)

2 limes, cut into wedges

In a caldero (stockpot), bring water to a boil. Add chicken breasts, chicken thighs, and salt and reduce the heat and simmer until chicken is tender, about 30 minutes. Remove chicken from broth, allow to cool, and then shred and set aside. Set aside the pot of chicken broth.

Heat 1 tablespoon of olive oil over high heat and fry the torn chile pieces quickly for about 1 to 2 minutes on each side. Be careful not to burn the chiles or it will have a bitter taste. Set aside.

Preheat the broiler and roast the tomatoes on a cookie sheet for about 20 minutes, turning over after 10 minutes to get all sides. Tomatoes should be mushy and slightly charred when ready. Remove only the charred pieces of skin.

(CONTINUED)

CHICKEN TORTILLA SOUP
(CONTINUED)

Puree the roasted tomatoes, fried chiles, onion, and garlic in a blender. Put the remaining 2 tablespoons of olive oil in a deep pot over high heat. Add the blended ingredients and fry for about 5 minutes. Add the chicken broth and simmer for 30 minutes.

Add the shredded chicken (or whole chicken and thigh pieces) and simmer for another 10 minutes. Add additional salt and some black pepper to taste.

In a large skillet, heat the canola oil over medium-high heat and fry the tortilla strips until lightly browned around the edges, about 45 seconds. Transfer the strips to paper towels to drain.

In separate serving bowls set out the cubed avocados, shredded cheese, shredded cabbage, and lime wedges.

Ladle the soup into bowls and top with a handful of tortilla strips. Each person can add some cubed avocados, a squeeze of lime juice and, if desired, some shredded cheese and cabbage.

6 TO 8 SERVINGS

LENTIL SOUP
SOPA DE LENTEJAS

Mi mamá made lentil soup often, especially during Lent. Once I left home I started making this delicious soup for my children. Over the years I reworked the recipe to make it heartier with the addition of carrots, celery, tomatoes, and spinach. When I make this soup during the late winter or early spring, I always remember *mi mamá*; it was one of her favorite *caldos* (soups). Nowadays I see so many lentil soup recipes that sound delicious with exotic ingredients and additions, but I will always like this one, with simple ingredients that bring out the earthy flavor of the lentils.

2 cups raw lentils

10 cups water

1 tablespoon salt

1 tablespoon olive oil

½ cup chopped carrots

2 stalks celery, chopped

2 vine-ripened or roma tomatoes, chopped

½ cup chopped yellow onion

1 clove garlic, chopped

1 cup coarsely chopped spinach

Sort the lentils by removing any stray beans or foreign pebbles that are sometimes present. Rinse lentils in a colander with cool water.

Over medium heat, in a large stockpot, bring the water to a boil and add the salt. After the water begins to boil, add the rinsed lentils and lower the heat. Cover and simmer until the lentils are almost tender, about 15 minutes.

While the lentils are cooking, heat oil in a large skillet over high heat. Add carrots, celery, and tomatoes and sauté for about 5 minutes. Add onion and sauté until translucent, about 2 minutes. Add garlic and sauté for 1 minute. Reserve.

Using a potato masher, mash the lentils coarsely to desired consistency. Add sautéed vegetables and simmer for 15 minutes. Add spinach and mix. Salt to taste.

Ladle into a big bowl and serve with your favorite bread.

8 TO 10 SERVINGS

HOMINY AND TRIPE SOUP
MENUDO

 *Menudo*—the breakfast of champions! Nothing else will do after a long night of celebrating. Christmas Eve, New Year's Day, and cold winter days are my favorite times to have *menudo*. Only a few women in our family have attempted Grandma's highly sought-after recipe, partly because we weren't sure where to begin and partly because of the number of hours needed to prepare it. If you have time and lots of patience and know the reward of this delicious recipe, then *menudo* awaits your valiant effort. *Menudo* tastes best topped with the perfect blend of chopped onions, crushed oregano (releasing its aromatic oils), a sprinkling of crushed red peppers, and a pungent squeeze of *limón*. Thank you, Mom, for keeping Grandma's recipe alive.

5 pounds smooth beef tripe, cut into 1-inch pieces

3 ox feet

5 pig's feet

18 cups water, divided

14 cloves garlic, chopped, divided

½ white onion, quartered plus 1 whole white onion, quartered

2 tablespoons salt, divided

6 cups Red Chile Sauce (page 25)

1 (6-pound) can white hominy, drained

2 teaspoons dried Mexican oregano

GARNISHES

1 large white onion, chopped

Lime wedges

Dried Mexican oregano

Crushed red chile

1 dozen bolillos or mini French bread rolls

Trim off excess fat from the tripe and cut into bite-size pieces. Thoroughly rinse tripe, ox feet, and pig's feet.

In a large (at least 10-quart) pot, over high heat, put 8 cups water and the ox feet, half the chopped garlic, the ½ onion, and 1 tablespoon of salt. Let it come to a boil uncovered. After it starts to boil, lower heat, cover, and simmer for 3 hours.

(CONTINUED)

RED PORK AND HOMINY STEW
(CONTINUED)

PREPARE PORK:

Place the pork and water in a slow cooker. Cook on low for 8 hours. Remove the pork and coarsely shred the meat. Skim the fat from the broth; you'll have about 2 cups of broth. Reserve.

MAKE SOUP:

In a blender, combine half of the oregano, red wine vinegar, chicken broth, pork broth, garlic cloves, onion, flour, and sea salt, and liquefy. Place the broth mixture into a very large (at least 14-quart) pot or divide recipe into two 8-quart pots. Repeat blending process with remaining oregano, red wine vinegar, chicken broth, pork broth, garlic, onion, flour, and sea salt and add to pot.

Add shredded pork, red chile sauce, drained hominy, and water to the pot. Partially cover and bring to a boil. Taste and add more red sauce, a bit at a time, to adjust the spice level to your liking. Lower the heat and simmer for 45 minutes. If necessary, season with salt.

Spoon pozole into soup bowls. Let your guests add the garnishes to suit their own taste. Serve with fresh or toasted bolillos (rolls).

MAKES ABOUT 12 QUARTS, 40 TO 48 SERVINGS

Note: Pozole keeps very well—even improves in taste over several days while refrigerated.

entrees

BEEF SHORT RIBS
COSTILLAS DE RES

 Every once in a while I crave short ribs prepared with liquid smoke surrounded by four basic vegetables: potatoes, carrots, corn, and onions. Less is more and this simple recipe is a winner in our home every time. My Grandma used to add bone marrow to this dish and my brother and I would fight over who was getting the larger piece. The buttery flavor of the marrow, spread over a warm corn tortilla and lightly salted, is an acquired taste. Even if you don't eat the marrow by itself, you should add it to the main dish for the incredible *sabor* it will give this dish.

4 pounds beef short ribs

2 or 3 bone marrow bones (optional)

1 tablespoon olive oil

8 ounces liquid smoke (recommend Claude's Barbeque Brisket Marinade Sauce)

3 red potatoes, quartered

2 carrots, peeled and quartered

2 ears of corn, quartered

1 teaspoon crushed dried Mexican oregano

1 teaspoon dried parsley

1 teaspoon salt

½ teaspoon ground black pepper

2 bay leaves

1 fresh rosemary sprig

½ yellow onion, sliced

Preheat oven to 350 degrees F. Arrange all the ribs and bone marrow bones, if using, in a roasting pan, casserole dish, or Dutch oven.

Pour olive oil and liquid smoke over the ribs. Surround the ribs with potatoes, carrots, and corn. Sprinkle the oregano, parsley, salt, and pepper over the meat. Place the bay leaves and rosemary sprig on the meat. Place the onion slices on the meat.

Cover roasting pan or casserole dish with aluminum foil or oven safe lid and bake for 2 to 2½ hours.

Remove the foil or lid and turn the meat over. Replace the foil or lid and bake for an additional 15 to 20 minutes. The ribs are done when you grab one of the rib bones and try prying it off the meat and it is loose and spins with little or no resistance. Remove the bay leaves before serving.

4 TO 6 SERVINGS

BEEF BRISKET TACOS
TACOS DE CARNE DESHEBRADA

Beef brisket is one of the easiest recipes to prepare when using a slow cooker. Just set up your slow cooker, add all the ingredients, turn it on, close the lid, and walk away. When you come back in 8 to 10 hours the meat just falls apart and is ready for the tacos. Mom always made beef brisket when we had a family get together and now I know why—it's easy, delicious, and she would always use the leftover brisket to make another family favorite, shredded beef *flautas* (page 157).

2 to 4 pounds beef brisket, fat trimmed

2 ounces liquid smoke per pound of meat (recommend Claude's Brisket Marinade Sauce)

2 bay leaves

12 ounces beer

Salt to taste

Ground black pepper to taste

12 to 24 corn tortillas (depending on how much you fill each taco)

Place the brisket, liquid smoke, bay leaves, and beer in a slow cooker. Cook on low for 8 to 10 hours.

Remove the brisket and shred the meat. Add salt and pepper to taste. Warm the corn tortillas. Place shredded brisket in tortillas and add your favorite toppings.

MAKES 12 TO 24 TACOS

TOPPING OPTIONS
Shredded cheese

Crema Mexicana or sour cream

Chopped cilantro

Chopped white onions

Avocados, pitted, peeled, and sliced

Salsa of choice

SHREDDED BEEF FLAUTAS
FLAUTAS DE CARNE DESHEBRADA

 When I first took my husband Steve home to meet my family, one of the meals Mom made was *flautas*. She presented us with a mountain of *flautas*, and Steve being from California called them "*taquitos*." And we all said, "No, *FLAUTAS*!" Well you would have thought he had committed a cardinal sin (which in our home he had)—we call our rolled and deep-fried tacos *flautas*. Mom's *flautas* are the best because not only is the brisket smoky and delicious, but she cuts it into bite-size pieces before stuffing each tortilla with tons of meat. Don't forget to have this with some freshly made guacamole, a salsa of your choice, and crema Mexicana.

Beef Brisket (page 155)

12 to 24 corn tortillas, depending on how much you fill each flauta

1 cup canola oil (for frying tortillas)

Toothpicks

TOPPING OPTIONS

Guacamole (page 117)

Salsa of choice

Crema Mexicana or sour cream

The beef brisket gets cooked for 8 to 10 hours. Once the meat is cooked and shredded, cut it into small bite-size pieces. Put the meat back into the brisket juices and allow the meat to soak up all the juices.

Warm corn tortillas on a comal (griddle) so they are pliable. Add some shredded brisket down the center of the tortillas. Roll the tortillas tightly and then add a toothpick to each to keep them rolled.

In a deep pan or deep fryer heat the oil over high heat until it is very hot. Carefully drop the flautas into the hot oil. Fry just long enough for the tortillas to get crispy and a light golden color. Turn over at least once using tongs and then drain upright on paper towels to allow excess oil to drain. Serve immediately with toppings.

MAKES 12 TO 24 FLAUTAS

CHICKEN TINGA
TINGA DE POLLO CON CHIPOTLE

Next time you're entertaining and want to keep your menu simple try chicken *tinga*. My sweet friend Cesi introduced me to her treasured family recipe. With a few tweaks this recipe delivers a wonderful authentic Mexican flavor, the number one criterion in our *familia*. I love setting up a *tostada* bar, where I provide a table filled with freshly made or store-bought *tostadas*, chicken *tinga*, and lots of toppings, and then I let my guests create their own magic.

6 cups water

2 pounds skinless, boneless chicken breasts

4 teaspoons salt, divided

1 whole clove garlic

1 medium yellow onion, quartered

1 large vine-ripened tomato, quartered

1 (7-ounce) can chipotle peppers in adobo
sauce

¼ cup canola oil

1 large yellow onion, chopped

3 large vine-ripened tomatoes, chopped

1 clove garlic, chopped

12 corn tortillas or packaged flat tostada shells

Oil for cooking tostadas

TOPPINGS (OPTIONAL)

1 head iceberg lettuce, finely shredded

3 avocados, pitted, peeled, and sliced

2 cups queso fresco or Cotija cheese,
crumbled

2 cups crema Mexicana or sour cream

2 cups salsa of your choice

6 radishes, sliced

In a large stockpot, over medium to high heat, add water, chicken, 2 teaspoons salt, whole clove garlic, and quartered onion. Cover and simmer for about 30 minutes. Remove the chicken, garlic, and onion from the broth and allow to cool. When the chicken is cool, shred it. Reserve chicken and broth.

In a blender, put the boiled onion and garlic clove, the quartered tomato, chipotle peppers including adobo sauce, 2 teaspoons salt, and enough chicken broth to fill the blender half way. Puree until smooth.

Heat the oil in a large and deep pan over medium heat. Once it is hot but not smoking, stir in the chopped onion and cook until soft and translucent, about 2 minutes. Add chopped tomatoes and chopped garlic and cook for an additional 2 minutes.

Add the shredded chicken, the chipotle sauce from the blender, and more chicken broth if it is too dry. Bring to a boil, reduce heat, and simmer for 20 minutes. Add salt to taste.

PREPARE TOSTADAS:

In a heavy skillet heat one-quarter inch of oil. Drop tortillas carefully into hot oil, one at a time, and fry for 20 to 40 seconds on each side or until crisp and golden. Drain on paper towels.

ASSEMBLE:

To assemble, place a tostada (fried tortilla) on a serving plate; spoon on some Chicken Tinga, lettuce (optional), 1 or 2 slices of ripe avocado, crumbled queso fresco, and top with crema Mexicana or sour cream. Garnish tostada with other toppings of your choice.

VARIATIONS: This recipe can also be used as a filling for flautas (page 157), gorditas (page 178), and tacos.

10 TO 12 SERVINGS

PORK RIND TACOS
TACOS DE CHICHARRÓN

Chicharrónes are a delicacy from Mexico; in particular, the northeast region of Mexico along the Texas border. Mexican street food inspires all sorts of unique recipes for food-on-the-go, and foods like corn in a cup (page 115) and tacos are some of my favorites. As a little girl I remember Mom selling burritos at the garment factory where she worked to help make ends meet. Burritos de *chicharrón* were one of the easiest and most flavorful burritos she made. This is that same *chicharrón* recipe she made for the burritos but served on soft, warm corn tortillas topped with chopped onions, cilantro, and a squeeze of lime. For a complete meal serve with a side of *frijoles de la olla* (page 215) and Mexican rice (page 223). *Aye que rico!*

1 tablespoon olive oil

⅓ cup chopped yellow onion

1 tablespoon all-purpose flour

1 cup Salsa Casera (page 60)

1 cup water

2 to 3 ounces plain chicharrónes (pork rinds), broken into bite-size pieces

Corn tortillas

TOPPINGS

Chopped onions

Chopped cilantro

Lime wedges

Heat oil in a non-stick skillet. Add onion and cook until translucent, about 2 minutes.

Add flour and cook for another 2 minutes while stirring. Add the salsa casera and cook until it boils.

Add the water and chicharrónes and let come to a boil again and then remove from the heat.

Allow the chicharrones to absorb the salsa before serving, about 30 minutes.

Heat corn tortillas on a griddle. Fill with the chicharrónes and serve with chopped onions, cilantro, and a squeeze of lime juice.

MAKES 2½ CUPS

GREEN CHILE WITH BEEF AND POTATOES

CHILE VERDE CON CARNE Y PAPAS

This recipe is a perfect example of how *mi mamá's* legendary homemade *salsa casera* could be transformed into a completely different recipe with the addition of just a few other ingredients. *Salsa casera* with some meat and potatoes makes a *delicioso chile verde con carne y papas*. I make this dish often because it's so simple to make and so comforting. It can be eaten as an entrée or used as a topping over burritos or *chile rellenos*. Garnish this dish with *rajas* and serve with homemade flour tortillas, *frijoles de la olla* (page 215), and *arroz* (page 223)—*aye que rico!*

1 tablespoon canola oil or shortening

2¼ pounds stew beef, diced

3 medium russet potatoes, diced

1 teaspoon salt plus additional to taste

5 cloves garlic, minced

1½ tablespoons flour

1½ cups Salsa Casera (page 60)

2½ cups water

Heat oil in a large skillet. Place the beef, potatoes, and 1 teaspoon salt in the skillet and cover and cook for about 10 minutes, until meat is cooked and potatoes are tender.

Uncover and add garlic and cook for an additional 2 minutes. Add flour and stir at least 2 minutes. Add salsa and water and stir. Let mixture come to a boil. Add additional salt to taste. Lower the heat and simmer for 5 minutes.

6 SERVINGS

PORK IN RED CHILE SAUCE
ASADO DE CHILE COLORADO

Mi mamá used to make this recipe during the winter when green chiles weren't in season or as fresh. As a result we ate more red chiles during the winter and green chiles during warmer weather. *Asado* is another name for this pork in red chile sauce. When I was a little girl, this was traditionally made outside on an open fire pit in a copper kettle. I remember running around the fire to keep warm as I waited anxiously for the *asado* to be done. Either pork or beef can be used, although pork lends a fuller flavor.

This pork in red chile sauce goes well with homemade corn tortillas (page 41), *frijoles de la olla* (page 215), and *arroz* (page 223). It's another hearty and comforting meal *mi mamá* would sometimes serve on Sundays.

2 tablespoons olive oil

2½ pounds pork loin roast, cut into 1-inch cubes

2 teaspoons salt

3 cloves garlic, chopped

4 cups Red Chile Sauce (page 25)

1¼ cups tomato sauce

¼ teaspoon dried Mexican oregano, crushed

⅛ teaspoon ground cumin

Water

Heat a large skillet over medium-high heat. Add oil to pan; swirl to coat. Add pork to pan; cook 5 minutes. Add salt and garlic and continue cooking until pork is thoroughly cooked, about 10 to 15 minutes.

Add red chile sauce, tomato sauce, oregano, and cumin. Let mixture come to a boil and add water to desired consistency. Simmer for another 10 minutes to let the flavors come together.

8 TO 10 SERVINGS

CORN FLOUR BOATS WITH PORK IN RED CHILE SAUCE
SOPES DE ASADO

Sopes are like an open-face taco, except thicker. My Grandma used to make these but called them *chalupitas* (little boats). She usually made these when she had leftover *asado de chile colorado* (pork in red chile sauce) and would fill each one with a tablespoon of *asado* and some *frijoles de la olla*, and top each with asadero cheese, then place them in the oven to let the cheese melt. You can top *sopes* with anything, but this is our favorite.

SOPES

2 cups masa harina (corn flour)

¼ teaspoon salt

1 tablespoon shortening

1¼ cups warm water

FILLINGS

4 cups Asado de Chile Colorado (page 167)

4 cups Frijoles de la olla (page 215)

1 cup shredded asadero cheese

Avocado slices (optional)

In a mixing bowl combine the masa harina and salt. Add the shortening and rub in with your fingers so that it is evenly distributed. Add warm water and knead until mixture is smooth and slightly sticky. If the dough is dry add more water, 1 tablespoon at a time. Dough should be soft and moist like play-doh and not dry. Divide dough into 8 portions. Cover with a damp cloth to keep the dough soft and moist.

Line a tortilla press with plastic wrap. Place a ball of dough on the press and cover with another piece of plastic wrap and press down to form a little ¼-inch-thick patty. Peel off the plastic wrap. (If you don't have a tortilla press you can use a heavy skillet or pot to make the dough patties or use your hands to form a patty.) Repeat with remaining balls of dough.

Preheat an ungreased comal (griddle) on medium-high heat. Cook a patty on the comal for about 2 to 4 minutes on each side until dry. While the cooked patty is still warm and as soon as you are able to handle it, pull the dough of the patty up and outward towards the edge, creating a little ridge of dough all the way around the circle to create a little "boat" or sope. Repeat with the remaining patties.

FILLING THE SOPES:

Preheat oven to 350 degrees F. Place sopes in a single layer on a baking sheet. Fill each sope with some warm asado and some frijoles, and sprinkle with cheese. Bake in the oven for 10 minutes. Garnish with avocado slices (optional).

TO MAKE AHEAD:

Cook sopes as directed. Place cooled sopes in a single layer in an airtight container, cover, and tightly seal. Sopes can be stored for one week in the fridge or in the freezer for one month. If frozen, allow to defrost before filling. Fill and bake as directed above.

MAKES 8 SOPES

CHIPOTLE SHREDDED PORK ENCHILADAS

ENCHILADAS DE PUERCO CON CHILE CHIPOTLE

Necessity is the mother of invention and this one was invented on the fly for sure. One day I had a big craving for red enchiladas (page 177), but unfortunately my pantry was low on red chile pods. That's when I spotted the solo can of chipotle peppers in adobo sauce. My hungry mind started racing about how to turn this can of peppers into some kind of enchilada sauce. Well you guessed it—that little can and a few other ingredients made a smoky-spicy chipotle sauce and a remarkably tasty pile of enchiladas. My husband suggested we add shredded pork, which was a match made in heaven. This sauce is spicy. If you are not a fan of too much spice, then use half the can of chipotle peppers or add an additional can of tomato sauce.

PORK

1 (2 pound) pork tenderloin

1 bay leaf

1 can (12 ounces) beer

SAUCE

2 roma tomatoes

4 tomatillos, husks removed, rinsed

1 (14.5-ounce) can diced tomatoes

1 (7-ounce) can chipotle peppers in adobo sauce

1 (8-ounce) can tomato sauce (depending on spice tolerance you may need an extra can)

½ large white onion, chopped

2 cloves garlic

1 tablespoon all-purpose flour

½ cup water

1 tablespoon olive oil

Salt to taste

ENCHILADAS

½ cup canola oil, for frying

12 to 18 corn tortillas, preferably white

1 medium white onion, diced

1½ cups crumbled queso fresco

½ cup crema Mexicana or sour cream, for topping

(CONTINUED)

CHIPOTLE SHREDDED PORK ENCHILADAS
(CONTINUED)

PREPARE PORK:
Place the pork tenderloin and bay leaf in a slow cooker; pour the beer over the meat. Cover and cook on low until well cooked and the pork shreds easily, 6 to 8 hours. Discard the bay leaf. Remove the pork from the slow cooker and shred the meat. Set aside for assembly.

ROAST TOMATOES AND TOMATILLOS:
Arrange tomatoes and tomatillos on a baking sheet. Place your oven rack as close to the broiler as possible. Broil the tomatoes and tomatillos for about 10 minutes until softened, turning over after 5 minutes. If the skins have blackened remove them.

MAKE SAUCE:
In a blender, puree the roasted tomatoes and tomatillos, canned diced tomatoes, chipotle peppers with adobo sauce, tomato sauce, chopped onion, garlic, flour, and water until smooth.

Heat olive oil in a large skillet. Pour in blended sauce carefully to avoid too much splatter and bring to a boil. Lower heat and simmer for about 10 minutes.

Taste and season with salt, usually about 2 teaspoons. If sauce is too spicy, add an additional can of tomato sauce and stir. If sauce is too thick, add water until desired consistency is reached, making sure to add more salt if necessary.

ASSEMBLE ENCHILADAS:
In a large skillet, heat canola oil until hot. Fry tortillas until softened. Drain on paper towels. Place lightly fried tortillas, one at a time, in the skillet of warm red sauce, turning to coat.

Place a coated tortilla on serving plate. Layer the chile-coated tortilla with some shredded pork, diced onion, and crumbled cheese. Place another coated tortilla on top and repeat layering until the stack has 3 tortillas. Continue making stacks until all tortillas are used. Serve each stack with a dollop of crema or sour cream.

VARIATION: OVEN-STYLE ENCHILADAS
Our family prefers our enchiladas stacked, but if you are cooking for a large group, oven-style might be the way to go.

Preheat oven to 350 degrees F. Spread 1 cup of the sauce in an ungreased 9-by-13-inch baking dish.

Fry tortillas in hot oil just until softened. Drain on paper towels. Fill with cooked pork, cheese, and onion. Roll tortillas and place seam side down in baking dish side by side in a single layer.

Pour 2 cups of the sauce over enchiladas. Sprinkle with more crumbled cheese. Bake until warm, about 15 to 20 minutes. Garnish with dollops of crema or sour cream and serve with your favorite side dish.

4 TO 6 SERVINGS

Time Saver: Cook your pork in a slow cooker all day and shred the pork that evening.

GREEN ENCHILADAS
ENCHILADAS VERDES

If I had to pick ONE recipe to remember Mom by this would be it. This is Mom's signature dish: delicious, spicy, stacked green enchiladas. We pile them flat and high, sometimes three and four tortillas high. After leaving home I craved her *enchiladas verdes* constantly and tried for years to duplicate them. Two ingredients make them uniquely her recipe, slow-roasted long green chiles and *suero de sal* (whey). The only place I know to get *suero de sal* is from Licon Dairy in El Paso, Texas. Buttermilk is a close second if I can't get my hands on *suero*. The combination of the *suero* with green chiles gives this recipe its one-of-a-kind *sabor*. Feel free to enjoy these stacked or rolled (as pictured).

SAUCE

12 Anaheim chiles, roasted and peeled (see
    page 20)

2 tablespoons flour

1 quart Suero de Sal (whey) or buttermilk,
    divided

Salt to taste

½ cup crema Mexicana or sour cream

½ cup canola oil for frying

12 to 18 corn tortillas, preferably white corn

1 pound shredded store-bought rotisserie
    chicken (optional)

1½ cups white shredded cheese (Monterrey
    Jack, asadero, or Muenster)

1 medium white onion, finely chopped

2 green onions, chopped (optional)

2 avocados, pitted, peeled, and sliced
    (optional)

In a blender combine the roasted and peeled
chiles, flour, and half the suero or buttermilk and
blend until creamy.

Pour mixture into large skillet and set over
medium-low heat to warm. Add remaining
suero or buttermilk and stir. Taste and season
with salt, usually about 2 teaspoons.

If the sauce is too spicy, add ¼ cup of crema
Mexicana or sour cream and stir. If the sauce is
too thick, add water until desired consistency is
reached.

ASSEMBLE STACKED ENCHILADAS:

In a non-stick frying pan heat canola oil. Drop
1 tortilla at a time into the hot oil and fry until
softened, turn once during frying. Drain on
paper towels. Soften tortillas by soaking in chile
sauce in skillet one at a time.

Place a chile-coated tortilla on a serving plate.
Layer with some shredded chicken (optional),
shredded cheese, and chopped onion. Top
with another coated tortilla. Repeat layers for
a total of 3 tortilla layers per serving. Serve
stacks with a dollop of crema Mexicana or sour
cream, some chopped green onion, and slices
of avocado.

VARIATION: OVEN-STYLE ENCHILADAS

Preheat oven to 350 degrees F. In a non-stick
frying pan heat canola oil. Drop one tortilla at
a time into the hot oil and fry until softened,
turning once during frying. Drain on paper
towels.

Spread 1 cup of the sauce in an ungreased
9-by-13-inch baking dish.

Fill each tortilla with some shredded chicken,
shredded cheese, and chopped onion. Roll
tortillas with filling and place seam side down
in the baking dish in one layer. Pour 2 cups
of the sauce over enchiladas. Sprinkle with
more cheese and bake until warm, about 15
minutes.

Serve with a dollop of crema Mexicana or sour
cream, chopped green onions, and slices of
avocado.

4 TO 6 SERVINGS

STACKED RED ENCHILADAS
ENCHILADAS ROJAS MONTADAS

 Our family usually prepares our red enchiladas *montadas* (stacked) topped with a fried egg. When I was a young girl I would watch my uncle Carlos eat his enchiladas with an over-easy egg placed on top. I finally had the courage to ask him if I could have a taste. It was love at first bite. The luscious yolk running down the stack of enchiladas gives this dish a unique flavor. With or without an egg, you'll find yourself making this recipe time and time again. Serve with *frijoles de la olla* (page 215) and *arroz* (page 223) or *macarrones con queso* (page 225).

1 tablespoon olive oil
4 cups of Red Chile Sauce (page 25)
Salt to taste
1 (8-ounce) can tomato sauce (optional)
½ cup canola oil for frying tortillas
24 to 32 corn tortillas, preferably white corn
1½ cups shredded Colby cheese
1 medium white onion, finely chopped
8 eggs (optional)

Heat olive oil in large skillet. Pour chile sauce into skillet and stir. Taste and season with salt if needed. If the sauce is too spicy, add a small can of tomato sauce and stir. If the sauce is too thick, add water until desired consistency is reached, making sure to add more salt if necessary.

In a non-stick frying pan heat canola oil. Drop 1 tortilla at a time into the hot oil and fry until softened, turning once during frying. Drain on paper towels.

ASSEMBLE ENCHILADAS:
Place lightly fried tortillas into the skillet of warm red sauce, one at a time. Coat the tortillas with the red enchilada sauce and place coated tortillas on a plate with a large slotted spoon.

Layer a chile-coated tortilla with some shredded cheese and chopped onion. Put another coated tortilla on top and repeat the layers until you have a stack of 3 to 4 tortillas. Continue to make stacks of tortillas until all ingredients are used.

Heat a small non-stick skillet over medium-low heat. Fry the eggs over-easy and place one on each stack of enchiladas—optional, but oh so worth the try.

8 SERVINGS

CORN FLOUR POCKETS
GORDITAS

 *Mi mamá* used to make these delicious *gorditas* (corn pockets) for us at home and also made them for our local Catholic Church bazaar with the *Guadalupanas* (Female Christian community devoted to the Virgin Mary). She would help at the annual bazaars for at least eight hours at a time and she did this up until the age of 90. The long lines at the *gordita* food booth were a testament to their popularity. Everyone knew they were worth the wait.

1 small Yukon Gold potato, peeled and cubed

1 teaspoon salt, divided

2 cups masa harina (corn flour)

1½ cups warm water

2 cups canola oil (for frying)

Filling of choice (see note next page)

TOPPINGS
Shredded lettuce

Chopped tomato

Shredded cheese

Salsa of choice

Crema Mexicana or sour cream

Boil diced potato in boiling water with ¾ teaspoon salt until soft enough to mash, about 15 minutes. Strain, mash, and set aside.

In a separate bowl, mix together the corn flour, water, ¼ teaspoon salt, and 1 cup mashed

potatoes. Knead for about 5 minutes. Cover with a dish towel and let stand for about 15 minutes.

Divide dough into 12 equal portions. Using your hands make 12 patties about ⅛ inch thick.

In a deep frying pan, such as a wok, heat cooking oil until very hot. Gently drop 2 or 3 gorditas into the oil. They will sink to the bottom of the pan. Once they rise to the surface, about 3 to 5 minutes, turn them over. Allow to cook for another 2 to 3 minutes. They should be a golden brown. Place the fried gorditas on paper towels to drain excess oil. Finish cooking all the gorditas and allow them to cool off slightly, about 5 minutes.

Cut open one end of each gordita creating a pocket. Fill with your filling of choice. Top filled gorditas with your choice of toppings. Enjoy the explosion of flavors as you bite into a gordita.

MAKES 12 GORDITAS

BEEF TONGUE WITH TOMATO
LENGUA ENTOMATADA

Lengua (beef tongue) is a delicacy that mi mamá would make with green chile. It must be boiled for several hours, making it quite tender. Once it's boiled all you do is sauté it with onions, garlic, and tomatoes, allowing the lengua to just melt in your mouth. She would make it occasionally on Sundays, when the family would visit after mass. My daughter Veronica came up with the idea to fill gorditas with lengua. The *lengua entomatada* tucked into the gorditas is a uniquely delicioso combination.

(CONTINUED)

Note: Gorditas can be filled with almost anything you have on hand. I guess you can say they are the Mexican pita. The most common filling at fiestas or bazaars is picadillo (page 181), or you can try filling them with papas con chorizo (page 185), tinga de pollo (page 160), or lengua entomatada (this page).

BEEF TONGUE WITH TOMATO
(CONTINUED)

2½ to 3 pounds beef tongue

3 cups water

1 small onion, quartered

5 cloves garlic

2 teaspoons sea salt

Gorditas (page 178)

SAUCE:

1 (14.5-ounce) can peeled or diced tomatoes

1 tablespoon olive oil

⅓ cup chopped white onion

1 tablespoon all-purpose flour

¼ teaspoon ground black pepper

½ teaspoon garlic powder

PREPARE TONGUE:

Place beef tongue, water, onion, garlic, and sea salt in a slow cooker. Cook on low for 6 to 8 hours.

Once it's tender, take the tongue out of the stock to cool off. Peel off the outer layer of skin when you are able to handle the tongue. It's easier to take the skin off while the tongue is warm. Dice tongue into ½-inch cubes and set aside.

Strain the stock and set aside. It's always better to refrigerate the stock so you can skim the fat off and discard. If you have a fat separator then you don't have to refrigerate.

MAKE SAUCE:

Puree tomatoes in a food processor or blender and set aside.

In a large skillet, heat oil over medium heat. Add onion and sauté until translucent, about 2 minutes. Add flour and stir for 2 minutes. Add pureed tomatoes and let come to a boil as you stir.

Add diced tongue, ½ cup reserved stock, black pepper, and garlic powder. Lower heat and simmer for 5 minutes to thicken. If it's too dry you can add more stock, however, this recipe should not be runny if using for filling gorditas.

If using for gorditas, fill each gordita with about 1 to 2 tablespoons of the prepared tongue and garnish with cilantro.

VARIATION: This recipe can also be used to make a beef lengua chile stew by adding more stock and ½ cup salsa casera (page 60).

MAKES 3 CUPS

GROUND BEEF AND POTATOES
PICADILLO

Picadillo was one of the first meat recipes I learned to make. We didn't have a lot of money growing up and ground beef seemed to be the meat of choice in our home since it was pretty inexpensive. I remember Mom said, "*Mira*, you just chop some onions, brown them, add meat and *papas* and you have a quick meat dish for anything." Well, it was a little more than that, but not too much more. We got fairly skilled at adding all sorts of other ingredients to this very basic *picadillo* recipe, and you will too. This quick and easy dish is the perfect filling for burritos or *gorditas* (page 178).

1 tablespoon olive oil

½ cup chopped white onion

1 pound ground beef

2 cloves garlic, minced

1 teaspoon salt

1 cup chopped roma tomatoes

1 small russet potato, peeled and finely chopped

In a large skillet heat oil over medium heat. Add onion and cook for about 2 minutes, until translucent.

Add ground beef and brown. Using a potato masher, mash meat so you have small pieces of meat with no big chunks. Drain off excess grease.

Add garlic, salt, tomatoes, and potatoes and cook over low heat for about 15 minutes, until potatoes are done. Salt to taste.

MAKES 3½ CUPS

STUFFED BELL PEPPERS WITH GROUND BEEF AND POTATOES
PIMIENTOS RELLENOS CON PICADILLO

The first time I ever ate stuffed peppers was at my *Tia* Victorina's house back on Riverside Drive in El Paso. I was about seven when I walked into her home while her stuffed bell peppers baked in the oven. The sweet fragrance of peppers baking overwhelmed my senses. When I inquired about it, she said, with her signature smile and quick laugh, "It's stuffed peppers, have you never had one?" To which I quickly replied, "No." "Sit down and I'll give you one." I ran, not walked, to the table and she gave me a plump pepper filled with *picadillo*. The combination was a perfect melody of sweet and savory. I think I may have swooned. I devoured it. Her husband (my Uncle Wolfgang) loved them so much he literally licked his plate clean. He and I giggled at his plate licking antics until my *tia* made him stop. To this day every time I make them, I think of her and that special day. This is my take on that little stuffed green pepper I ate so many moons ago. *Gracias Tia Victorina*.

3 bell peppers (your choice of color)

1 batch Picadillo (page 181)

1 tablespoon olive oil

½ cup crumbled queso fresco

Cilantro, for garnish (optional)

Preheat oven to 350 degrees F.

Make picadillo for stuffing the bell peppers.

Rinse the peppers. Cut the tops off and remove the white flesh and seeds. Rinse out the inside of each pepper. In a large stockpot parboil the peppers, about 3 minutes. Remove the peppers and drain any excess water that is inside them. Brush each pepper with olive oil.

Heat up a comal (griddle) and place the peppers on their side on the comal, about 1 minute on each side, just long enough to sear the sides of each pepper.

Prepare a baking dish (about 10.5 inches by 7 inches) that will accommodate your 3 peppers. Spray the dish with cooking spray to keep the peppers from sticking to it. Pour about ¼ inch water into the dish.

Stuff each pepper with some picadillo and place in the baking dish. Cover with foil and crimp the edges onto the dish creating a seal. Bake for about 25 to 30 minutes.

Remove from the oven and let rest for about 5 minutes. Plate 1 pepper per plate, top with crumbled queso fresco, and garnish with cilantro. For a complete meal, serve with Cilantro Lime Rice (page 221) or Black Bean Salad (page 213).

MAKES 3 STUFFED BELL PEPPERS

POTATOES AND MEXICAN CHORIZO
PAPAS CON CHORIZO

Papas con chorizo is my quick go-to meal for breakfast, lunch, or dinner. If I have it for breakfast I scramble it with eggs and serve it rolled up in a warm flour tortilla. If it's an appetizer I want then I serve it with *tostadas* or on mini *sopes*. If I want to make *papas con chorizo* for dinner I just make some *gorditas*, stuff them, and serve with some *frijoles de la olla* (page 215) on the side. All around it is a quick, easy, and lightly spicy dish packed with bold flavors.

2 tablespoons kosher salt, divided

5 Russet or Yukon Gold potatoes, washed, peeled, and cut into ¼-inch cubes

10 ounces Mexican chorizo, casings removed

1 cup shredded queso quesadilla cheese

Preheat oven to 350 degrees F. Bring about 8 cups water to a boil in a deep pot with 1½ tablespoons of salt. Carefully add potatoes to boiling water. Boil over medium-high heat for about 15 minutes. Check at 10 minutes. If they are tender but not firm then remove from the heat. You do not want to overcook the potatoes. Using a colander, strain the potatoes but do not rinse.

While the potatoes are cooking, crumble the chorizo into a cast-iron skillet or a casserole dish. Cover with foil and place in the preheated oven for about 15 to 20 minutes. Check after 10 minutes. The chorizo will release some oil but don't discard it. (You can always cook the chorizo in a nonstick pan on the stovetop but I prefer this method because it makes less of a mess.)

Add the cooked potatoes to the cooked chorizo along with the remaining ½ tablespoon of salt to taste and gently combine. Do not stir too much or the potatoes will get mushy. Top with the shredded cheese. Place back in the oven, uncovered, just long enough for the cheese to melt.

Serve with tostadas, mini sopes (page 168), warm corn or flour tortillas (page 41 and 43), or use as in photo to fill gorditas (page 178).

10 SERVINGS

CHILE BEANS WITH MEXICAN CHORIZO

FRIJOLES ENCHILADOS

I started making this recipe while I was working two jobs. It was a great go-to meal for my kids after school. When I had leftover *frijoles de la olla* and red chile sauce I would simply add chorizo and ground beef to create this simple dish. Serve this in big bowls with saltine crackers or *galletas* (page 47) and you have a great cold weather or game day meal.

1 pound ground beef

12 ounces Mexican chorizo, casings removed

2½ cups Frijoles de la Olla with liquid (page 215)

1½ cups Red Chile Sauce (page 25)

1 cup water

½ teaspoon dried Mexican oregano

Salt to taste

Shredded Colby cheese (optional)

Spray a large heavy skillet with nonstick cooking spray and set on moderately high heat until hot but not smoking. Add the ground beef and brown for about 10 minutes. Drain off any excess grease.

Add the chorizo by crumbling it into the cooked ground beef. Cover the skillet and cook the chorizo thoroughly for another 5 to 10 minutes. Using a potato masher, combine the beef and chorizo together.

Transfer to a large pot and add the frijoles and liquid and cook for 5 minutes. Add the red chile sauce, water, and oregano and cook until it starts to boil, stirring occasionally. Reduce heat to low and simmer, uncovered, for about 10 minutes. Add more liquid from beans if mixture is too thick.

Add salt to taste. Ladle into bowls and sprinkle with a handful of cheese.

8 TO 10 SERVINGS

CHILE RELLENOS TOPPED WITH RANCHERO SAUCE

CHILE RELLENOS CON SALSA RANCHERA

Chile rellenos are roasted long green chiles made from Anaheim or poblano chiles, stuffed with cheese or meat, breaded in flour, and dipped in egg whites, then quickly deep fried to perfection. These are some bold chiles. They take some time to make but are so worth the effort.

Mom used to make *chile relleno* burritos and sold them at the garment factory where she worked. I distinctly remember her waking up at around four in the morning to make them from scratch. Her *chile relleno* burritos were quite popular. She always sold out when she made them. As a single mother raising three kids, she was extremely resourceful at finding ways to make ends meet. If you've never tried one, now's the time, and they don't get any better than Mom's. The smokiness of the roasted chile, light breading, and melted cheese will sell itself right into your heart's palate.

RANCHERO SAUCE

2 chiles güeros

1 tablespoon olive oil

1 cup chopped white onion

½ celery stalk, chopped

3 small tomatoes, chopped

1 clove garlic, minced

1 tablespoon all-purpose flour

1½ cups water

Salt to taste

Freshly ground black pepper to taste

1 teaspoon chicken broth granules

CHILE RELLENOS

12 large Anaheim or poblano chiles, roasted and peeled (see page 20)

4 cups shredded Monterey Jack, Muenster, quesadilla, or asadero cheese

1 cup white all-purpose flour

2½ teaspoons salt, divided

1 teaspoon ground black pepper, divided

8 eggs, separated

¼ teaspoon cream of tartar

2 cups canola oil for frying

1 avocado, pitted, peeled, and sliced (optional)

(CONTINUED)

CHILE RELLENOS TOPPED WITH RANCHERO SAUCE
(CONTINUED)

MAKE RANCHERO SAUCE:

Boil chiles güeros until soft. Remove stems and chop. Heat olive oil in a saucepan and sauté onion, celery, and boiled chiles for 3 minutes.

Add tomatoes and garlic, and sauté for an additional 3 minutes. Add flour and stir for 2 minutes.

Add water, salt, black pepper, and granules and simmer about 5 to 10 minutes.

MAKE CHILE RELLENOS:

After roasting and peeling the chiles, carefully remove the stems and pull out the membranes and seeds being careful not to tear the chiles. Fill each chile through the stem opening with some cheese and set aside.

On a plate combine flour, ½ teaspoon salt, and ½ teaspoon black pepper. Place the filled chiles in the flour and coat all sides well. Shake off any excess flour. Reserve.

Note: Dip each chile one at a time into the egg batter and only right before frying. You will need to work quickly during this process so the egg batter doesn't fall off. It's best to work with a large saucepan so you can fry about 2 to 3 chiles at the same time.

Using an electric hand mixer beat the egg whites and cream of tartar on high speed until soft peaks form. In a separate bowl, mix together the egg yolks, 2 teaspoons salt, and ½ teaspoon pepper. Carefully fold the egg yolk mixture into the egg whites being careful not to mix too much so the egg whites don't fall.

Fill a large heavy-bottomed saucepan about a third of the way up with canola oil and heat on medium-high heat. You want to get the oil very hot before frying your chile rellenos. Test the oil by dropping some of the egg white mixture into the oil. If the mixture sizzles and floats to the top, it's the right temperature. If it sinks, the oil is not hot enough.

Dip the filled and flour-dusted chiles into the egg mixture until well coated, forming a little cocoon. Coat each chile one at a time just prior to frying. Carefully place the egg-coated chile rellenos in the hot oil, about 2 at a time. Fry until golden brown, turning once. Drain on paper towels. Change paper towels 2 to 3 times to absorb excess oil.

Arrange the chile rellenos on a serving platter and drizzle each with some warm ranchero sauce and serve.

MAKES 12 CHILE RELLENOS

CHEESE AND SHRIMP STUFFED POBLANOS

CHILE RELLENOS DE CAMARON Y QUESO

If you love *chile rellenos* like I do, then you'll love this recipe. It's actually a healthier version of a traditional *chile relleno* that still packs a bold Mexican flavor. If you want the good old traditional egg-battered deep-fried recipe, that one is on page 189, but I encourage you to give this one a try too. Poblanos are readily available at grocery stores year-round, which makes this dish a welcoming dinner choice for any time of year. It's also a filling and flavorful meat-free meal during Lent.

8 poblano chiles, roasted and peeled (see page 20)

2 tablespoons olive oil

1 pound medium shrimp, peeled, deveined, and chopped

½ teaspoon salt, divided

5 cloves garlic, minced

1½ tablespoons all-purpose flour

¼ teaspoon ground black pepper

½ cup crema Mexicana or sour cream

¾ cup fat-free milk, divided

¾ cup (3 ounces) shredded quesadilla cheese

1 red bell pepper, roasted, peeled, seeded, and chopped

2 tablespoons chopped cilantro

2 tablespoons fresh lime juice

½ cup queso fresco, crumbled

Pomegranate seeds (optional)

Using a small sharp knife, carefully slit roasted chiles open along one side. Remove seeds, leaving stems attached. Set aside to fill later.

PREPARE THE FILLING:

Heat a large skillet over medium-high heat. Add oil to pan and swirl to coat. Sprinkle shrimp with ¼ teaspoon salt. Add shrimp to pan; cook 3 minutes or until done. Remove from pan and reserve.

Add garlic to pan; sauté 30 seconds, stirring constantly. Add flour and ground black pepper; cook 1 minute, stirring constantly. Slowly add crema Mexicana, stirring with a whisk. Stir in ½ cup milk; cook 1 minute, stirring constantly. Remove from heat; let stand 2 minutes.

(CONTINUED)

CHEESE AND SHRIMP STUFFED POBLANOS

(CONTINUED)

Add quesadilla cheese and ¼ teaspoon salt
and stir until smooth and cheese melts. Place
⅓ cup of cheese mixture in a large bowl;
reserve remaining cheese mixture.

Add cooked shrimp, roasted bell pepper,
cilantro, and lime juice to the ⅓ cup cheese
mixture; toss to coat.

TO SERVE:

Stir remaining ¼ cup milk into reserved cheese
mixture. Spoon 3 tablespoons of this cheese
sauce onto each of four plates.

Stuff each poblano chile with 6 tablespoons
shrimp mixture. Place 2 stuffed poblanos onto
each plate with cheese mixture and garnish
with crumbled queso fresco, some cilantro,
and pomegranate seeds (optional).

MAKES 8 STUFFED POBLANOS

PAN-FRIED TILAPIA WITH MANGO AND AVOCADO SALSA
TILAPIA CON SALSA DE MANGO Y AGUACATE

Growing up we did not eat much seafood, but as I grew older and started eating it more often, I quickly fell in love with it and made up for lost time. This recipe is quick and easy to make. The flavor is delicate yet complex enough to entice the palate. The sweet mango and avocado salsa pairs well with the simply prepared tilapia, making it a memorable and healthy meal. Add a side of cilantro lime rice (page 221) and this beautiful dish will be sure to impress.

1 pound tilapia fillets

⅓ cup all-purpose flour

1 teaspoon garlic powder

1 teaspoon ground black pepper

¼ teaspoon salt

3 tablespoons salted butter

Mango and Avocado Salsa (page 55)

Rinse tilapia fillets and pat dry with paper towels.

Mix flour, garlic powder, pepper, and salt in a shallow dish. Dip fillets in flour mixture and coat both sides.

Heat butter in skillet over medium heat until hot. Add floured fillets to skillet and pan fry for 3 to 4 minutes on each side or until golden.

Place fillets on a platter and spoon the mango and avocado salsa over fish before serving.

4 SERVINGS

SPICY MUSHROOM TORTA WITH CHEESE

TORTA DE HONGO CON RAJAS Y QUESO

Tortas are quick and easy sandwiches made with *bolillos*. You can make them cold or grill the bread before stuffing. This grilled mushroom *torta* oozes creaminess, and the addition of long green chiles and tequila gives it just the right dimension of smokiness. The tequila notes linger on one's tongue just long enough to taste the fumes from the agave. Give this *torta* a try on a cold winter night or cool summer evening.

2 tablespoons salted butter, divided

½ tablespoon olive oil

1 cup sliced mushrooms

Salt to taste

Ground black pepper to taste

5 tablespoons sour cream

3 Anaheim chiles, roasted (see page 20), peeled, stemmed, and cut into ½-inch strips

3 teaspoons tequila (optional)

½ cup shredded queso quesadilla cheese, divided

2 bolillo rolls (oval Mexican sandwich rolls) or French bread rolls

Melt 1 tablespoon butter with olive oil in a medium skillet over medium heat. Stir in mushrooms and sauté for 10 minutes or until tender. Add salt and pepper to taste. Add the sour cream and chile strips and cook until warm. Remove pan from heat.

Carefully add tequila. Return to heat and simmer, uncovered, for 1 minute or until most of the tequila has dissipated. Stir in ¼ cup cheese until melted. Set mixture aside.

Preheat a comal (griddle) or panini press. Split rolls in half and coat both the inside and the outside of each roll with the remaining butter. Brown the inside of each roll. Layer the bottom roll with the warm mushroom and chile mixture, top with some shredded cheese, and add the top half of the roll.

Grill the sandwiches over moderate heat, turning once, until the bread is lightly toasted and the cheese has melted, 5 to 6 minutes. If using a panini press, close the lid and press down slightly using even pressure. Most sandwiches cook perfectly on a panini press in 2 to 3 minutes.

MAKES 2 TORTAS

HAM AND AVOCADO TORTA

TORTA DE JAMÓN Y AGUACATE

 *Tortas* are very easy to make and perfect for summer. I used to make and sell them in our family grocery store (Soza's Grocery). Everyday I would make at least a dozen and they would sell out by noon. I made them with fresh asadero cheese which I bought at a local dairy. Freshly made cheese is the best and what I think makes these *tortas* so good. But you can make them using your favorite slice of cheese and it will be just as tasty.

4 bolillos (oval Mexican sandwich rolls) or other sandwich rolls

4 tablespoons mayonnaise

4 to 8 thin slices deli ham

4 slices asadero cheese

1 large avocado, pitted, peeled, and sliced

1 tomato, sliced

Romaine lettuce

4 jalapeños peppers (optional)

Slice the bolillos in half lengthwise, not cutting all the way through. Open the rolls and spread about 1 tablespoon of mayonnaise on the inside of each.

On each roll, place 1 to 2 slices of ham, 1 slice of cheese, some avocado and tomato slices, and lettuce. Serve with a fresh jalapeño.

MAKES 4 TORTAS

REFRIED BEAN TOSTADAS AND GUACAMOLE TOSTADAS

TOSTADAS CON FRIJOL Y TOSTADAS CON AGUACATE

If you have corn tortillas, then you can make *tostadas*. All you have to do is fry them until crisp. You can even purchase pre-packaged *tostadas*, making this a quick and tasty dinner. My kids love topping their own *tostadas* on Friday family nights when we stay home and watch movies or play games. Our favorite toppings are refried beans and guacamole. If you're like me and you have a mishmash of leftovers from the week, just reheat leftover chicken, meat, or pork, cut it into bite-size pieces and top your *tostadas* with the toppings of your choice. This meal is perfect for those of us who can't stand to throw food away, just like Mom and Grandma.

REFRIED BEANS

2 tablespoons olive oil or vegetable shortening

1½ cups cooked Frijoles de la Olla plus ½ cup liquid (page 215)

Salt to taste

TOSTADAS

8 corn tortillas or 8 pre-packaged tostada flats

Vegetable oil for frying

TOPPINGS

Guacamole (page 117)

Shredded lettuce (optional)

Chopped tomato

Queso fresco or cheese of choice

Salsa of choice

MAKE REFRIED BEANS:

Heat the olive oil in a medium skillet over medium-high heat. Add the beans and the liquid. Cook over medium heat. While the beans are boiling mash them with a potato masher. Continue to cook until they form a thick paste, about 10 minutes. Season to taste with salt.

FRY TORTILLAS:

In heavy skillet, over high heat, heat one-quarter inch of oil. Lower heat to medium and fry tortillas, one at a time, in hot oil for 20 to 40 seconds on each side or until crisp and golden. Drain on paper towels. Store bought tostadas can also be used.

MAKES 8 TOSTADAS

ASSEMBLE TOSTADAS:

Top 4 tostadas with guacamole and 4 with
refried beans. Top each with lettuce, tomato,
and cheese. If you want a heartier tostada add
bite-size pieces of cooked chicken, pork, or beef.
Drizzle with your favorite homemade salsa.

CHILAQUILES ROJOS

Whenever we had red enchiladas (page 177) and there happened to be leftover red sauce, which wasn't often, I could always count on having *chilaquiles* for breakfast the next day. *Chilaquiles* are fried corn tortilla pieces covered with red chile sauce and topped with cheese, then served with eggs, any style. The fried tortilla is usually a little crunchy, which is a nice change from its cousin the red enchilada. It's my quick, go-to breakfast whenever I'm craving red enchiladas early in the morning. Because *chilaquiles* are one of my favorite things to have for breakfast, sometimes I make a double batch of red chile sauce just to ensure there's some leftover.

8 corn tortillas

1 tablespoon canola oil

2 cups Red Chile Sauce (page 25)

1 cup shredded queso quesadilla or Colby cheese

⅓ cup diced green or red onions

4 to 8 eggs, cooked any style

Cut corn tortillas into quarters. In a large skillet heat oil and fry corn tortilla pieces until crunchy. Lower heat to low.

Add red chile sauce and mix only long enough to coat all the tortillas. Top with cheese while still over low flame and cook just long enough for cheese to melt.

Remove from heat and sprinkle with onions. Serve with eggs any style.

4 SERVINGS

OLD-FASHIONED MEXICAN OATMEAL

AVENA

Warm *avena* (oatmeal) was one of the breakfast meals *mi mamá* would prepare for us before school, especially during the winter. Today, instant oatmeal can simplify things, but I have to say there is something different about homemade oatmeal prepared on a chilly morning. I prefer a smoother, less chunky oatmeal, and the best way to prepare it is by cooking it longer than the directions call for. Oatmeal flavored with cinnamon is a great breakfast for people with high cholesterol and/or diabetes, as oatmeal has a high fiber content and cinnamon has been shown to help glucose levels. When you puree it in the blender it becomes an *atole*, smooth oatmeal, which is a good way to prepare it for the elderly and the very young. It was *mi mamá's* favorite when she got older and my grandson Hunter won't have it any other way.

8 cups water

3 cinnamon sticks

¼ teaspoon salt

2 cups old-fashioned oats

1 cup low-fat sweetened condensed milk

Ground cinnamon (optional)

Sugar (optional)

Honey (optional)

In a saucepan bring the water with the cinnamon sticks to a boil. Remove from heat, cover, and let steep for 1 hour. Discard the cinnamon sticks.

Add salt and oats to the water and let it come to a boil uncovered. Lower heat and simmer for 30 minutes, stirring frequently to prevent sticking. Add milk and simmer for an additional 15 minutes until creamy.

Serve in a bowl and add more milk or water if you want it thinner. Sprinkle with cinnamon and sweeten with sugar or honey. Refrigerate leftovers for up to 1 week.

MAKES 8 TO 9 CUPS

sides

POTATO SALAD
ENSALADA DE PAPA

Mom's famous potato salad was and still is requested at family barbecues, weddings, and baby showers. It has quite the following. One time she used 40 pounds of potatoes. Knowing our hard-working mother, she probably peeled all 40 pounds in one day. The ingredients come together nicely when made 24 hours before serving. The first time I made it, it didn't taste quite like Mom's so I called her to find out what was missing. It was then she revealed her secret weapon: pickle juice. I'll never forget to include it again!

2½ pounds Yukon Gold or red potatoes, peeled and diced

1 tablespoon salt

1 to 2 cups mayonnaise

2 tablespoons yellow mustard

2 tablespoons pickle juice

½ teaspoon ground black pepper

¼ cup chopped green onions

1 cup chopped celery

½ cup chopped dill or sour pickles

4 ounces pimientos, drained and chopped

5 eggs, hard-boiled, peeled, and chopped

Salt to taste

Boil potatoes in salted water to cover over high heat, about 15 minutes. Do not cover the pot. Strain the potatoes but DO NOT rinse. Spread potatoes in a single layer on a shallow pan to allow them to cool off. Once potatoes are cool, cover pan with foil and put in the fridge for about 4 hours or overnight to completely chill. This will prevent them from getting mushy when adding the other ingredients.

In a large mixing bowl mix the mayonnaise, mustard, pickle juice, and black pepper. Add the green onions, celery, pickles, and pimientos. Add the cooled potatoes and diced eggs and combine all the ingredients gently, you don't want this salad to get mushy from too much mixing. Add salt to taste.

MAKES 8½ CUPS

MANGO, JICAMA, AND CUCUMBER SALAD

ENSALADA DE MANGO, JICAMA, Y PEPINO

Mangos are decidedly my favorite tropical fruit. With their warm yellow hue, fragrant aroma, and juicy flesh, mangos seems to call to me every time I pass them on the street or in the produce section of my grocery store. I love eating a mango on its own, but I've found it also plays nicely with other fruits. Take this salad for instance; mangos, jicama, and cucumber sprinkled with some fresh lime juice and dusted with a little red chile powder. Your mango just went from delicious to unforgettable. Make it at least a few hours ahead so all the luscious flavors have time to meld.

2 small yellow mangos, peeled, pitted, and cut into ½-inch cubes

2 red or green mangos, peeled, pitted, and cut into ½-inch cubes

1 medium jicama, peeled and cut into ½-inch cubes

1 medium cucumber, peeled, seeded, and cut into ½-inch cubes

2 to 3 tablespoons lime juice

⅛ teaspoon chile powder or fruit and snack seasoning (recommend Tajin Fruit and Snack Seasoning)

Dash of cayenne pepper

Salt to taste

In a mixing bowl combine the mangos, jicama, cucumbers, and lime juice. Sprinkle with chile powder, cayenne pepper, and salt.

Toss well, cover, and refrigerate for at least 1 hour before serving.

8 TO 10 SERVINGS

BLACK BEAN SALAD
ENSALADA DE FRIJOLES NEGROS

Several years ago we were having a cookout and I made too much *pico de gallo*. Not knowing what to do with it I decided to add some black beans and canned corn to the leftover salsa. After tasting it and tweaking it some more, such as adding diced avocados and red onions, I finally got the taste I was looking for. So here you have it, one of my favorite light, quick, and easy cold salads. Just be sure to double the batch for parties—it goes quickly!

⅓ cup red wine vinegar

⅓ cup extra virgin olive oil

⅛ teaspoon ground cumin

¼ teaspoon ground coriander

Juice of 1 lime

1 tablespoon salt

1 teaspoon ground black pepper

2 (15-ounce) cans black beans, rinsed and drained (or 4 cups freshly cooked black beans)

4 roma tomatoes, seeded and chopped

½ red onion, finely chopped

Handful cilantro, chopped

1 (15-ounce) can corn, drained

½ serrano pepper, finely chopped (optional)

1 avocado, pitted, peeled, and cubed (optional)

In a small bowl make the dressing by combining the red wine vinegar, olive oil, cumin, coriander, lime juice, salt, and ground black pepper.

Put the black beans in a large bowl. Add the tomatoes, red onion, cilantro, corn, and serrano pepper, if using. Add the dressing and toss. Add avocados, if using, and toss gently.

Chill salad for about 30 minutes or overnight to marinate. Mix one more time before serving.

10 SERVINGS

PINTO BEANS
FRIJOLES DE LA OLLA

 Mom always said, "If there are *frijoles* in the house, then you have something to eat." Beans are a true staple in Mexico. Freshly made *frijoles de la olla* is my favorite way to have beans. There is nothing more pure and earthy than the taste of homemade pinto beans. My kids love bean burritos, but there are so many ways to use *frijoles*. You can eat them straight out of the pot, hence the name *frijoles de la olla*, and you can have them mashed or refried. If you like refried beans try frying them in lard, like Grandma did, or in bacon or sausage drippings, or mash them up with some Mexican chorizo. The possibilities are endless.

2 cups dried pinto beans

¼ onion, sliced (optional)

Salt to taste

Spread the beans over your counter so you can look for any pebbles or beans that are broken, discolored, or shriveled and remove them.

Place beans in a colander. Rinse thoroughly with cool water for about 3 minutes. This step is not necessary, but your beans will be lighter in color and "mas bonitos" as my Mom says.

Soak the beans in cold water in a covered bowl for 4 to 6 hours before cooking. (I never soak them and they still come out bonitos. I think they come out bonitos when the beans are fresh, so I prefer to be a rebel and skip this step.)

Drain the beans and pour into a large pot. Add enough water to come 3 inches over the beans. Bring to a boil over medium-high heat. Cover and simmer until the beans are tender, about 3 to 4 hours, adding more hot water as the beans absorb liquid. (Every pot is different so check your beans after 2 hours. Most take 3 to 4 hours but I have a pot I love to cook my beans in because it only takes 2 hours.) Add salt and onions, if using, about 1 hour before cooking is complete.

Refrigerate beans in any liquid left when cooled. Beans can be refrigerated for up to 5 days. The beans can also be frozen in small bowls for later use.

6 SERVINGS

ZUCCHINI WITH CORN
CALABACITAS CON ELOTE

This has to be one of the oldest dishes in Mexican homes. According to Grandma, everyone used to have a garden in their yards, even a small one, and, along with corn, squash was one of the staples harvested. Squash is bountiful in the summer and fall and so we had *calabacitas con elote* quite often while I was growing up. This is one of those recipes I find myself longing for whenever I see all the squash varieties available. The buttery creaminess of the *suero* catapults me to my childhood every time.

8 ears of corn, shucked

1 tablespoon olive oil

1 small onion, chopped

3 cloves garlic, minced

4 zucchini or Mexican squash, chopped

2 cups suero (whey) or buttermilk

Salt to taste

Ground black pepper to taste

1 cup shredded white cheese (Chihuahua or
   Monterrey Jack)

Remove corn kernels from the cobs using a knife on an angle. Set kernels aside.

Heat the olive oil in a large skillet over medium-high heat. Sauté the onion in the hot oil for about 2 minutes. Add the garlic and sauté for 1 more minute until fragrant.

Add zucchini and corn and cover and cook until zucchini is tender, about 10 minutes.

Uncover and add the suero or buttermilk. Season with salt and pepper and stir. Bring to a boil. Reduce heat to low and simmer about 10 minutes.

Sprinkle with cheese before serving, if desired.

6 TO 8 SERVINGS

JALAPEÑOS WITH SOY SAUCE
CHILES TOREADOS

These little chiles pack a lot of punch for being so small. The idea of this recipe is to give the jalapeños a heightened taste of smokiness by steaming them in a bath of butter and soy sauce. I really like this recipe, especially with a barbecued steak and grilled vegetables. If you like adding some spice to your Sunday afternoon barbecue, try making these the morning of your event to give your meal that little extra bite.

5 jalapeño peppers

2 tablespoons soy sauce

1 tablespoon salted butter

Preheat oven to 400 degrees F.

Place jalapeño peppers on a piece of foil and drizzle with soy sauce and butter. Wrap tightly and place packet on a cookie sheet. Bake for 12 to 15 minutes.

MAKES 5 CHILES

CILANTRO LIME RICE
ARROZ BLANCO CON CILANTRO Y LIMÓN

 I've always loved cilantro lime rice but we never made it growing up. I love the tartness of the lime and the bold flavor of the cilantro. I thought to myself I must learn to make this at home. So I went on a quest. I tried several recipes and still didn't quite get the flavor I was looking for. I eventually realized that basmati rice was the single ingredient that made all the difference. So after several trial-and-error sessions in my kitchen I finally got it right. My husband says this is his favorite rice now. The sugar softens the tartness of the lime juice and gives the overall recipe the balance I was looking for.

So here you have it, a simple cilantro lime rice that pairs exceptionally well with a hot and spicy dish. I especially like it with freshly grilled fish or a spicy *mole* dish (page 159). As much as I love my *arroz* (page 223), this recipe is a pleasant alternative to the tomato base used in Mexican rice.

1 tablespoon salted butter

1 cup uncooked long-grain white basmati rice

½ teaspoon granulated sugar

Juice of 1 to 2 small limes, divided

2 cups water

1 teaspoon salt

3 tablespoons chopped cilantro

In a saucepan over low-medium heat melt the butter. Add the rice and sugar. Mix briefly to coat the rice with the butter and sugar. Add half the lime juice and stir for 1 minute. Add water and salt.

Bring the rice to a boil over high heat. Reduce heat to medium-low, cover with a tight-fitting lid, and simmer until the rice is tender, 20 to 25 minutes.

Remove from heat and sprinkle the rice with the cilantro, the rest of the lime juice, and more salt if needed. Fluff rice with a fork. Cover and let sit for 5 minutes before serving.

4 SERVINGS

Variation: My daughter Veronica mixes in some frozen peas and carrots which gives it a wonderful taste and colorful presentation.

MEXICAN RICE
ARROZ A LA MEXICANA

This side dish is one of the first recipes I learned to cook when I was a little girl. It is a staple in most Mexican kitchens, and has such a wonderful aroma while it's cooking. I have to confess, however, that I had a few disasters while learning to make this dish. One time I cooked the rice without toasting it first; I thought it was just boiled like when *mi mamá* would make *arroz con leche*. I added some tomato sauce and thought I had done a darn good job, but oops, it didn't taste like the delicious one that *mi mamá* made. Even after she taught me how to make it, the rice would still come out sticky, overcooked, or a little bit crunchy. Finally, with enough practice, I mastered it, and now it's one of the easiest dishes I make. I'm sure it will be one of yours too.

1 tablespoon olive oil

1 cup long-grain rice

¼ cup chopped yellow onion

2 cloves garlic, chopped, or 1 teaspoon garlic powder

3 cups water or 2 cups water and 1 cup unsalted chicken broth (fresh or packaged)

⅓ cup tomato sauce

1 (3.1-ounce) cube tomato or chicken bouillon

Heat oil in a medium skillet over medium heat and add rice. Stir until rice is slightly browned. Remove skillet from the heat and add the onions and fresh garlic, if using. Stir until onions are translucent. (The pan is usually warm enough to cook the onions and fresh garlic, keeping them from burning.)

Add water, chicken broth, if using, tomato sauce, bouillon cube, and garlic powder, if using. Stir and let mixture come to a boil; lower heat, cover, and simmer for 10 minutes.

Stir gently after 10 minutes, cover, and let simmer for another 10 minutes. (If adding canned or frozen vegetables add them during the last 10 minutes.)

After the final 10 minutes of cooking, turn heat off, fluff rice with a fork and cover again for another 3 to 5 minutes so liquid can finish absorbing.

8 SERVINGS

MACARONI AND CHEESE
A LA MEXICANA
MACARRONES CON QUESO

I used to make this macaroni and cheese for my children all the time, and now I make it for my grandchildren. This recipe goes a long way and everyone loves it. There's nothing like homemade macaroni and cheese with a Mexican twist.

3½ cups water

2 teaspoons salt

1½ cups elbow macaroni

2 tablespoons chopped Spanish onion

2 cloves garlic, minced

1 tablespoon unsalted butter or olive oil

1 (8-ounce) can tomato sauce

2 teaspoons tomato bouillon

1½ cups shredded Monterrey Jack, Muenster, queso quesadilla, or asadero cheese

Bring water and salt to a boil in a medium saucepan. Add macaroni and boil for 12 minutes. Remove from heat and set aside, but do not drain.

In a large skillet, sauté onion and garlic in butter or olive oil for 2 minutes. Once onions are translucent add cooked macaroni with the water, tomato sauce, and bouillon and bring to a boil.

Turn off heat. Sprinkle cheese on top and cover until cheese melts. Best when served warm.

6 SERVINGS

VANGIE'S FAMOUS THANKSGIVING STUFFING
RELLENO PARA PAVO

 When I started making stuffing I was just 13 years old. I began with helping my older sisters by doing all the chopping. Over the years I changed some of the ingredients and finally came up with this recipe. Having made this recipe for years, it is engrained in my memory. *Mi mamá* loved my stuffing and so do my children and grandchildren. I usually double this recipe to give some away to neighbors or anyone else who doesn't cook at Thanksgiving; I usually include all the other fixings and a homemade pumpkin pie. They are always so grateful; the smiles on their faces warm my heart.

2 small pork chops

1 teaspoon salt

1 loaf (16 ounces) white bread slices

1 pound bacon

4 ounces Jimmy Dean premium pork sage sausage

2 medium tomatoes, chopped

1 small onion, finely chopped

1 (32-ounce) carton chicken broth (recommend organic low sodium), plus more if needed

2 sticks unsalted butter, plus another ½ stick for topping

1 carrot, peeled and shredded in a food processor

4 celery stalks, quartered and shredded in a food processor

1 (6-ounce) bag (from a 12-ounce box) Mrs. Cubbison's Classic Seasoned Dressing

1 (2.25-ounce) can diced black olives

1 teaspoon poultry seasoning

Ground black pepper to taste

(CONTINUED)

VANGIE'S FAMOUS THANKSGIVING STUFFING
(CONTINUED)

Boil pork chops in some water with 1 teaspoon salt added until cooked all the way through, about 20 minutes. When cool, chop into small ¼-inch pieces and then finely chop in a food processor and set aside. Reserve cooking water.

Toast bread slices on a cookie sheet in the oven or in a toaster and when cool tear into small ½-inch pieces and set aside.

Chop bacon into ½-inch pieces and fry in a large skillet until cooked but not crispy; drain and set aside. Discard the drippings.

In the same skillet, cook the sausage, breaking it up or mashing with a potato masher as it cooks. Drain and set aside.

In the same skillet used for cooking the bacon and sausage, sauté the tomatoes and onion about 5 to 7 minutes. Add chopped pork chops, cooked bacon, and cooked sausage and stir together and simmer for a few minutes allowing the flavors to come together. Remove from heat and set aside to cool.

In a separate large pot, combine the chicken broth, butter, carrots, and celery. Let come to a boil. Add 1 bag of dressing (there are 2 in the box) and mix well. Remove from heat. Allow to cool.

In a large bowl, combine toasted bread pieces with the sausage mixture and dressing mixture. If this is too dry add some pork chop water or chicken broth, a little at a time.

Add black olives, poultry seasoning, and black pepper to taste. Mix well, cover, and refrigerate overnight, allowing the flavors to incorporate.

Preheat oven to 350 degrees F. Place stuffing in a 9x11-inch greased pan and add 4 to 6 pats of butter on top of the stuffing. Cover with aluminum foil. Bake for about 1 to 1½ hours, uncovering the last 10 to 15 minutes.

VARIATION:
During Thanksgiving there are so many dishes that need oven time, you can always put your stuffing in a slow cooker. (Though I personally love the crunchy layer on the stuffing created the last 15 minutes in the oven.) If using a slow cooker, just spray slow cooker with non-stick cooking spray. Add stuffing and put 4 pats of unsalted butter on top of stuffing. Cook on high for about 1 hour until it gets to a boiling stage and bread expands, then lower temperature to low. This will keep it warm until it's ready to be served (make sure it doesn't burn on the sides).

20 SERVINGS

desserts

MEXICAN RICE PUDDING
ARROZ CON LECHE

I distinctly remember having a warm bowl of *arroz con leche y pasas* (with raisins) for breakfast before going to school, especially on a cold morning. Instead of using just evaporated milk, like *mi mamá* did, I changed her recipe a bit and added sweetened condensed milk. The wonderful memories of my brother Carlos and I sitting in our warm kitchen are still with me. I can still hear *mi mamá* telling us to hurry so we wouldn't be late for school.

3½ cups water

2 cinnamon sticks

3 to 5 whole cloves

¼ teaspoon salt

¾ cup long-grain white rice

¾ cup evaporated milk

½ cup sweetened condensed milk (recommend La Lechera)

1 cup dark raisins

1 tablespoon ground cinnamon, for sprinkling when serving

Over high heat, bring the water to a boil with the cinnamon sticks, cloves, and salt. Remove from the heat and cover. Steep for about 45 minutes to 1 hour.

Remove cinnamon sticks and cloves and discard. Add rice and over medium heat boil for 20 minutes.

Add the evaporated milk, condensed milk, and raisins and continue to cook over low heat for about 10 minutes. Stir gently but be careful not to stir too much so rice doesn't get mushy.

Ladle into bowls and sprinkle with cinnamon.

8 SERVINGS

MEXICAN BREAD PUDDING
CAPIROTADA

 Say the word *capirotada* to a Mexican and it conjures up all sorts of childhood memories. The aroma created by the ingredients in the sauce are quite unique because of the *piloncillo*, a pure, unrefined sugar that is pressed into a cone shape. *Piloncillo* tastes very similar to brown sugar with a more smoky molasses flavor. The smell of the *piloncillo* and spices simmering on Mom's stove lingered in her kitchen for hours. As a kid we always ate *capirotada* during Lent, but I know of families who eat it during Thanksgiving, *Navidad*, and *Las Posadas*.

The ingredients in this recipe carry a rich and symbolic religious representation for some Mexican and Mexican-American families. The bread is for the Body of Christ, the syrup is his blood, the cloves are the nails on the cross, the cinnamon sticks symbolize the wooden cross, and the melted cheese stands for the Holy Shroud. Hence why this is eaten during the Lenten season.

As great as *capirotada* smells fresh out of the oven, my favorite time to eat it is about two days after it's made. Sometimes I like eating it cold, straight out of the pan. The tanginess of the cheese, the sweetness of the *piloncillo*, and the added spices make this a *postre* (dessert) worth trying.

4 bolillo rolls or French rolls

4 tablespoons butter or spray butter

4½ cups water

12 ounces piloncillo or 1½ cups packed dark brown sugar

4 cinnamon sticks

6 whole cloves

1 cup raisins

3 cups shredded Longhorn Cheddar or Colby cheese

Preheat oven to 350 degrees F.

Cut rolls into ½-inch slices and butter both sides of each slice. Layer on a baking sheet and bake for 3 minutes on each side, until lightly toasted and dry. Remove and cool.

Combine water, piloncillo, cinnamon sticks, and cloves in a large saucepan. Bring to a boil; reduce heat, and simmer uncovered for 20 minutes, creating a syrup. Remove from heat, cover, and let steep for 2 hours. Pour through a strainer and discard cinnamon sticks and cloves. Set syrup aside.

Spray an 8-inch x 10½-inch baking dish with non-stick spray. Layer the ingredients in the following order: a third of the toasted bread, a third of the raisins, a third of the cheese, and then pour 1½ cups syrup evenly over cheese. Wait 15 minutes and then layer another third of the bread, raisins, and cheese, and pour another 1½ cups syrup evenly over cheese.

Let soak for another 15 minutes. Top with the remaining bread, raisins, and cheese, and pour remaining syrup evenly over bread. Let set for another 15 minutes.

Cover the dish with aluminum foil that has been sprayed with nonstick spray and bake 40 minutes. Uncover and bake until cheese is golden brown, about 10 to 15 minutes more. Serve warm.

8 TO 10 SERVINGS

COCONUT FLAN
FLAN DE COCO

The texture and taste of flan is similar to another one of my favorite desserts, crème brûlée. However, instead of a crystallized sugar coating and eating it from the ramekin, flan is turned out of the ramekin and served on a plate, allowing the amber-colored and caramelized sugar to ooze over the top and down the sides of the flan further enhancing its creamy texture. Flan is quite versatile. You can make it plain or give it a boost of flavor with a tinge of vanilla. And if you're even more adventuresome you can play with plain flan by adding some of your own favorite flavors. I especially love coconut and thought this would make a refreshing tropical flan. After lots of experimenting I finally got the sweet, light, and creamy coconut flavor I was looking for by using coconut milk. Stay away from coconut cream as it gives the flan a lumpy texture.

4 cups milk

1 cup granulated sugar, divided

3 eggs

3 egg yolks

1 tablespoon coconut extract

1 cup coconut milk

⅓ cup coconut flakes

Bring the milk and ½ cup sugar to a boil and mix well until the sugar has dissolved. Keep the mixture at a low boil for about 45 minutes, mixing occasionally during cooking time.

While you are reducing the milk, prepare the caramel: Put the remaining ½ cup sugar in a small saucepan over medium heat. Allow the sugar to melt, about 5 to 7 minutes. No need to stir, just swirl the saucepan around over the heat until it starts to melt. Once the sugar is a deep maple color it is ready. Quickly drizzle the caramel into the bottom of 8 4-ounce ramekins. The caramel will harden and crackle as it cools off. Don't worry, it will liquefy once it's in the oven with the flan.

(CONTINUED)

COCONUT FLAN

(CONTINUED)

Preheat the oven to 350 degrees F and place the oven rack in the middle of the oven. Beat the eggs, egg yolks, coconut extract, and coconut milk in a mixing bowl.

Strain the reduced milk into a separate bowl. (Straining will remove any solid particles or milk skins.) Quickly whisk the egg mixture into the reduced milk mixture. Slowly pour into the prepared ramekins.

Place ramekins in a roasting pan and put on the middle rack in the oven. Carefully add warm water halfway up the sides of the ramekins. Bake for 35 minutes or until edges are set (the centers will not be set).

Remove roasting pan from the oven and remove ramekins from the water and place on a wire rack to cool completely for at least 1 hour.

After 1 hour, cover ramekins with plastic wrap and transfer to the refrigerator and chill for at least 8 hours or overnight. (These can be made several days in advance and still taste delicious.)

When ready to serve, toast coconut in a dry pan just until it has a nice golden color. Carefully run a paring knife around edges of the ramekins to loosen the flan, invert onto serving plates, sprinkle with some of the toasted coconut and serve.

8 TO 10 SERVINGS

Note: Toast coconut in a warm skillet without any oil. It toasts quickly so don't leave unattended.

TRES LECHES PUMPKIN FLAN
FLAN DE CALABAZA Y TRES LECHES

One Thanksgiving my mother ordered a *tres leches* pumpkin flan from a friend that was unforgettable. Every subsequent Thanksgiving I found myself wishing I had that recipe. After experimenting I finally came up with my own. This pumpkin flan is rich and velvety, fragrant with traditional pumpkin-pie spices with the texture of a cheesecake. The cream cheese in this flan makes it firm and smooth while still soft and creamy. With any flan the trick is to cook it in a water bath to ensure gentle heat so it won't break or curdle. The consistency of the pumpkin in this recipe gives this flan a non-traditional flan texture. If you want a velvety texture then strain the mixture before you pour it into the bundt pan.

½ cup granulated sugar

8 ounces cream cheese, softened

2 eggs, room temperature

2 egg yolks, room temperature

1 (14-ounce) can sweetened condensed milk

1 (12-ounce) can evaporated milk

1½ cups milk

1 teaspoon pure vanilla extract

¾ cup fresh pumpkin puree or organic pumpkin puree from a can

½ teaspoon ground cinnamon

⅛ teaspoon ground cloves

⅛ teaspoon ground ginger

⅛ teaspoon ground nutmeg

Preheat oven to 325 degrees F. Spray a 10-inch bundt pan with cooking spray.

Cook sugar in a saucepan over medium heat, stirring often, 5 to 7 minutes or until melted and medium-brown in color. Drizzle the sugar mixture into the bundt pan and then swirl the caramelized sugar around to coat the bottom of the pan. (Because of the temperature change when coating the bundt pan, the sugar may harden quickly, don't worry, once the flan is added and baked it will liquefy into a beautiful golden syrup.)

(CONTINUED)

TRES LECHES PUMPKIN FLAN
(CONTINUED)

In a large bowl, beat cream cheese at medium speed with an electric mixer for 1 minute. Reduce speed to low and add eggs and egg yolks and beat until well blended. Slowly add all three milks and the vanilla, and beat at low speed for 1 minute.

Add pumpkin puree and spices and continue to mix for 1 to 2 minutes. Pour mixture into prepared bundt pan. (Mixture may be slightly lumpy. If you want a smooth flan then strain the mixture before you pour it into the bundt pan.)

Place bundt pan in a roasting pan. Place roasting pan on the center rack of oven and add hot water to the roasting pan to come halfway up the sides of the bundt pan. Bake for 1 hour and 20 minutes or until edges are set (the center will not be set).

Remove roasting pan from oven and remove bundt pan from water. Place on a wire rack and let cool completely for at least 1 hour.

Transfer to the refrigerator and chill for at least 8 hours or overnight.

Carefully run a butter knife around edges to loosen, and invert flan onto a serving platter.

8 TO 10 SERVINGS

BUÑUELOS

It just wouldn't be Christmas without these easy-to-make sugar and cinnamon treats. I love having *buñuelos* in the morning with a little *cafecito* during the holiday season. This is my Mom's recipe. Just remember to make all twenty because they go quickly. You can even stack them about three to five high, tie them with festive twine, and take them to the next Christmas gathering you attend. Your hostess will love you for it. They are irresistible, especially drizzled with *miel virgen* (honey) or *cajeta* (Mexican caramel). *Buñuelos* are crunchy and aromatic with the delicate scent of cinnamon and each sugary crunch whispers, "*Feliz Navidad!*"

3 cups all-purpose flour

1 teaspoon baking powder

1 teaspoon salt

1 teaspoon ground cinnamon

¾ cup milk

4 tablespoons unsalted butter

1 teaspoon pure vanilla extract

2 eggs

Canola or vegetable oil for frying

CINNAMON-SUGAR COATING

1 cup granulated sugar

1 teaspoon ground cinnamon

(CONTINUED)

PUMPKIN TURNOVERS
(CONTINUED)

ASSEMBLE AND BAKE EMPANADAS:
Preheat the oven to 350 degrees F.

Take out half the dough and split it into 12 equal balls of dough.

On a floured surface, roll out the dough balls into small round circles. Place a small dollop of pumpkin filling on one half of each of the dough circles. Wet the bottom edge of the circles with water to help seal the two halves. Fold over the dough to cover filling and seal off the edges with a fork by pressing down along the edges. This also makes for a pretty pattern when baked.

Repeat with remaining dough and filling.

Brush each empanada with some canned evaporated milk or egg whites, sprinkle with cinnamon and sugar mixture. Puncture the top of each empanada with a fork to allow steam to escape while baking.

Spray a large cookie sheet with cooking spray, place the empanadas on the cookie sheet and bake for 15 to 20 minutes on middle rack in the oven. If after 15 minutes you notice the bottoms of the empanadas starting to brown, move the cookie sheet to the top rack and continue to bake for the last 5 minutes, until golden brown.

Enjoy the empanadas warm or at room temperature. Refrigerate baked empanadas for a few days. Reheat in a toaster oven or bake at 350 degrees for 8 minutes.

MAKES 24 EMPANADAS

APPLE TURNOVERS
EMPANADAS DE MANZANA

 The house that my parents bought in El Paso was a three room house with four fruit trees in the backyard—apple, apricot, peach, and *membrillo* (quince). *Mi mamá* never let anything go to waste; she would preserve and can all the fruit. She sat for hours peeling piles of apples and then she would make warm apple pies and *empanadas*. Whenever I smell these *empanadas* baking, I envision *mi mamá* in the kitchen by my side humming and smiling. I have simplified the recipe to avoid cooking the apples first, and they come out just as tasty as *mamá's*.

4 cups chopped Granny Smith apples

2 tablespoons all-purpose flour

½ cup sour cream

1 teaspoon ground cinnamon

¼ teaspoon salt

1 teaspoon pure vanilla extract

1 batch Empanada Dough (page 254)

GLAZE
Canned evaporated milk or egg white

Cinnamon-sugar mixture (1 teaspoon ground cinnamon mixed with ¼ cup sugar)

Preheat the oven to 350 degrees F. Combine all ingredients except dough together in a large mixing bowl and set aside.

Divide empanada dough into 24 pieces. On a floured surface, roll out the dough pieces into small round circles. Place a small dollop of apple filling on one half of each of the rolled-out circles. Wet the edges of the circles with water to help seal the two halves. Fold over the dough and seal off the edges with a fork by pressing down along the edges. This also makes for a pretty pattern when baked.

Brush each empanada with some canned evaporated milk or egg whites, sprinkle with cinnamon-sugar mixture. Puncture the top of each empanada with a fork to allow steam to escape while baking.

Spray a large cookie sheet with cooking spray; place the empanadas on the cookie sheet and bake for 13 to 20 minutes on middle rack in the oven. If after 15 minutes you notice the bottoms of the empanadas starting to brown, move the cookie sheet to the top rack and continue to bake for the last 5 minutes, until golden brown.

MAKES 24 EMPANADAS

CARROT CAKE WITH
CREAM CHEESE FROSTING

Gracias a Dios que nos dio el pan de cada día,
sin merecerlo. Amén.
Thank you God for our daily bread,
we are undeserving. Amen.

Panza Llena, Corazón Contento
Full Stomach, Happy Heart

SPAN